STAND UP
SPEAK UP
START UP

The SCAD Guide for Creative Entrepreneurs

1
The Ally

Allies root for you — and studies show they will help your career.

2
The Believer

Entrepreneurs hold deeply personal ideas about how to make the world better.

3
The Hacker

Hackers challenge outmoded conventions in pursuit of breakthrough results.

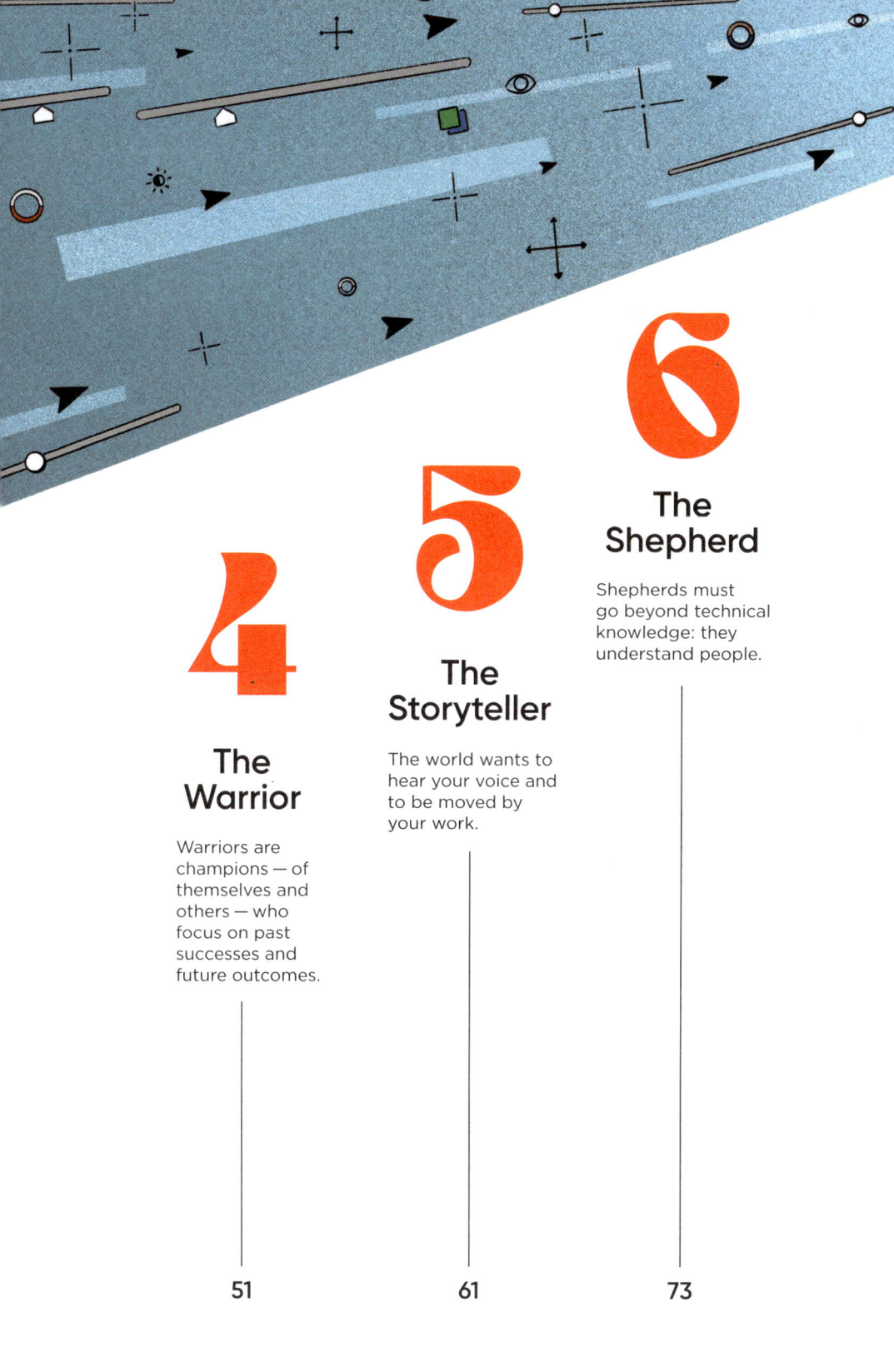

4

The Warrior

Warriors are champions — of themselves and others — who focus on past successes and future outcomes.

51

5

The Storyteller

The world wants to hear your voice and to be moved by your work.

61

6

The Shepherd

Shepherds must go beyond technical knowledge: they understand people.

73

Foreword

Back in 2005, I was a recently retired CEO of one of the largest fashion brands in the world and about to become (at the tender age of 60) an entrepreneur. I had the good fortune, at the time, to meet the ultimate entrepreneur, Paula Wallace.

Single-handedly, this gracious educator with an iron will had founded and developed SCAD, one of the most successful universities in the world. She saved Savannah, Georgia in the process and transformed the city into one of the most exciting and vibrant destinations in the US. She had also resurrected the European village of Lacoste, France, and was remaking Midtown Atlanta into a destination for creative entrepreneurs and students of entrepreneurship. I can think of no better person in the world to speak with authority on becoming an entrepreneur.

This new book from SCAD demystifies the concept of *entrepreneurialism* by showing how ambitious, creative, passionate young people already possess the essential quality of all successful startup founders and business leaders: the gift of invention. Each chapter explores how creative talents — such as the gifts SCAD students and graduates use to animate, design, tell stories, produce films, and more — can also be employed to launch a new startup and to add value to an existing business.

What I love most about this book is how SCAD so helpfully decodes the complexity of starting your own company by emphasizing and exploring those character traits essential to successful startup founders and creative professionals: The Ally, The Believer, The Hacker, The Warrior, The Storyteller, and The Shepherd. I've seen all six archetypes throughout my career — in my colleagues and competitors, and in myself, too! I can attest through personal experience that Paula Wallace and the expert educators of SCAD know this topic well. SCAD is the perfect destination for future entrepreneurs and those who wish to hire brilliant creative leaders.

— Domenico De Sole
CEO of Gucci Group (1994–2004)
Chairman of Tom Ford International (2005–present)

Welcome to the
School of Invention

by SCAD President and Founder Paula Wallace

The world has changed profoundly since the founding of SCAD almost fifty years ago, when our mission to prepare students for professional, creative careers was so far beyond the vision and imagination of more traditional universities. Others in higher education didn't know what to make of SCAD.

"Careers? For creative people?" many asked. To some, this was radical. But for students who wanted rewarding, lifelong careers using their gifts of invention, this was not radical. SCAD was, and is, the future.

"No starving artists!" was our battle cry.

SCAD has achieved remarkable results for students, families, and graduates who want to launch their own companies and contribute their talents to the world's biggest and most beloved brands. Career success is woven into every fiber of the university. SCAD grads revolutionize the notion of what you can do with a degree from an "art and design school," though that phrase does not reflect the full scope of a SCAD education. Think of SCAD as a "school of invention," because that is what our students do when they're here, and what they spend their careers doing when they graduate.

SCAD alumni work and lead at an astounding variety of companies. This includes many companies you'd expect, like Disney, Apple, Google, Meta, Amazon, NBC Universal, CNN, Nike, Louis Vuitton, Chanel, but there's also a remarkable list of companies and organizations you may not, like Deloitte, Delta Air Lines, Bank of America, Capital One, Goldman Sachs, 3M, Hewlett Packard, BMW, and Volvo. SCAD grads work across healthcare, the largest industrial sector in the world, as well as at NASA, the CDC, and the CIA. They also found and lead their own studios and startups in fashion, filmmaking, software development, agribusiness, accessory design, and more. You'll meet many such SCAD entrepreneurs in this book.

Mark Strassmann of CBS Evening News came to SCAD for a story on American innovation and asked me how we launch so many careers for creative graduates. "Where other universities prize tradition, SCAD leans into the future," I said. "Companies desperately need creativity — creativity that isn't abstract and isn't ethereal." Creativity,

I shared with Strassmann, is about relevant invention. "SCAD doesn't teach anything you can't get a good job in."

A 2022 study from Creatively reports that creative pros command an average annual salary of $156,000. Starving artists? Far from it.

When thinking about the tectonic shifts in business over the last few years, where more and more companies are seeing the need to hire creative talent, consider the words of *Shark Tank*'s legendary guru Kevin O'Leary. In 2021, when an interviewer asked him what degree provides the highest chance of success in a career, O'Leary remarked that three years earlier he would have said engineering.

"But I've changed my mind," he said. "Since the pandemic hit, the number one demand I have for my companies is for people that can take the concept of a business and tell a story about it, produce a video, do really rich photography."

He goes on to say that he's now paying his writers, editors, videographers, and photographers competitive six-figure salaries because they can solve business challenges with highly specialized tools and creative thinking.

For many, the word *entrepreneur* conjures up tech gurus, software developers, and "finance bros" in sporty vests, but that's far too limiting. Entrepreneurship is fundamentally about seeing opportunity where others do not — identifying needs in the market, pitching solutions to clients and colleagues, creating new products and services, and adding value to the bottom line. This visionary element is why creativity is so important to entrepreneurship.

Intrapreneurship, on the other hand, describes leaders and creatives who practice innovation not with their own startup but within a larger company or organization. All those SCAD grads working in finance, consulting, and healthcare, for example, are intrapreneurs.

ENTREPRENEURSHIP

is fundamentally about seeing opportunity where others do not.

LEADERSHIP

INTRAPRENEURSHIP

describes leaders and creatives who practice innovation, not with their own startup, but in a larger company or organization.

As you'll see in this book, most successful startup founders began their careers working for established companies. Entrepreneurs almost always begin as intrapreneurs. To master the art of both, a record number of students and families choose SCAD, because SCAD never stops innovating to keep pace with a changing world.

For example, we've recently created five new SCAD schools. The De Sole School of Business Innovation – Named for Domenico De Sole, a titan of business in the world of luxury brands and author of this book's foreword – prepares future leaders who understand the centrality of digital engagement for every client and customer on the planet. Marrying tech and entertainment, the School of Creative Technology is where students can create meaningful experiences, from Zuckerberg's Metaverse to Disney theme parks. The School of Film and Acting and the School of Animation and Motion equally benefit from two LED volume stages (i.e., technology used to create all those Marvel and Star Wars spinoffs on Disney+). Employment of actors is expected to grow 30% during this decade and roles for directors and producers are expected to grow over 20%, while employment for special effects artists and animators is projected to grow 16%. The deluge of new films and shows that comes with this growth will have all the storyboards and high-concept imagery they need thanks to our newly anointed School of Visual Communication.

These and six more SCAD schools (Building Arts, Design, Fashion, Fine Arts, Foundations, and Liberal Arts) prepare grads for the work of tomorrow, which is already happening today. We know SCAD degree programs are what Fortune 100 companies want because we ask industry leaders what they need. We've just launched our second degree program developed in partnership with Google, the new BFA in user experience research – a recognition that mobile apps are central to all our lives: banking, healthcare, coordinating rides to soccer prac-tice via GroupMe, you name it.

We also incorporate a Business Core into the general education curriculum required of every SCAD student. Every creative pro needs to understand contracts, marketing, and the language of business – from screenwriters negotiating with agents to architects opening their own studios.

More students than ever before dream of working for themselves and launching their own companies. In this book, SCAD experts draw on a wealth of wisdom and experience to describe how to make that dream a reality.

In each of the six chapters, you'll encounter an archetype — i.e., a specific character trait found in the lives of successful entrepreneurs. We've chosen to build this book around archetypes because so many of us at SCAD are inspired by the writings of Joseph Campbell. His classic works, such as *The Hero with a Thousand Faces*, have influenced nearly every blockbuster film of the last fifty years, from the myriad Star Wars spinoffs to each installment in the Marvel Cinematic Universe.

Campbell says every hero's journey begins with a Call to Adventure. You may already have received your call — the transformative idea that you want to bring forth into the world. Or perhaps you simply know that building a new brand or opening your own studio is your dream. SCAD can help you discover and develop the ideas that are already inside you.

Campbell's second step is Refusal, which you might be wrestling with right now. It's that little voice inside your head that questions whether you've got what it takes. Spoiler alert: you do. With a little help in the form of Supernatural Aid, Campbell's way of referring to a mentor, a guide who will help arm you with the skills you'll need on your journey. Your mentors eagerly await your arrival at SCAD. We surround our students with a dream team of mentors — our expert faculty, who come from the very industries our grads will transform — to guide them along their creative odysseys, coax out their innate inventiveness, and to help them discover the kind of entrepreneur they're destined to become.

The heroic entrepreneurial archetypes you encounter here include The Ally, The Believer, The Hacker, The Warrior, The Storyteller, and The Shepherd. SCAD is designed to help you cultivate strength in all six.

SCAD has an amazing support system to guarantee success for all current, former, and even future students. SCAD Career and Alumni Success offers a lifelong career coach for every student and graduate and helps students find allies. SCAD SERVE, the initiative that helps students change the world — in the areas of clothing, food, shelter, and the environment — awakens students to their strongest beliefs and how to apply their talents to making the world better for all.

SCADpro, our in-house research and design consultancy, partners students with leading companies, such as: Coca-Cola, Google, Disney, Amazon, Mercedes-Benz, and many others. These partnerships teach students how to become hackers and to realize revolutionary new ideas to solve real-world business challenges.

SCADpro Fund, which invests in alumni-owned companies, equips new SCAD grads to fight and win their startup battles and get their products to market. The SCAD Alumni Atelier and SCAD Art Sales do the same, funding product development residencies for alumni and selling student and alumni artwork to companies and private collectors. Our professional presentation studio, SCADamp, prepares students to be excellent storytellers by teaching them expert verbal, visual, and interpersonal communication techniques. The end result is a proven ability to connect with clients.

All of these resources teach SCAD students to become shepherds who lead talented teams toward success. Collaboration and teamwork are the lifeblood of every entrepreneur and a daily reality at SCAD. Every entrepreneur and intrapreneur is, by necessity, a shepherd.

SCAD's greatest contribution to the world is our people power, the collective genius and generosity radiating from our more than 65,000 students and alumni. They start at SCAD and then are hired and called to every corner of the map to build better, kinder, and more beautiful and just communities for all.

While the graduate with a "traditional" degree arrives at work on day one ready to learn, SCAD grads arrive ready to work. Whether you're a high school student preparing to choose your next adventure, a college student with entrepreneurial dreams, or a recent graduate already developing your first product for the market, it's time to stand up, speak up, start up!

Find a group of people who challenge and inspire you; spend a lot of time with them, and it will change your life.

— Amy Poehler

1

The Ally

One day, home on break from college, Eleanor found herself digging through boxes in the basement, looking for old family photos and vintage finds. At the time, she was also looking for ideas about her future career. As a fashion major, she had a dizzying array of options. Should she try and work in Paris or Milan? Stay in the US and work for one of the big brands, like Target or Levi's? These were the questions on her mind when she found a curious little object inside one of the boxes: a small brass button stamped with three words, "The Big Favorite."

"Do you know what this is?" she asked her dad, later that day.

"I sure do." He went on to explain that his grandfather, Eleanor's great-grandfather, had been a textiles and manufacturing entrepreneur in the earliest years of the twentieth century. His grandfather founded a company called The Big Favorite, which produced workwear, overalls, and other denim products for the nation's farmers and laborers. Eleanor was fascinated. The button seemed full of enchantment and magic. In that moment, she saw that fashion and entrepreneurship were "literally in my blood."

Soon after, Eleanor landed a summer internship with Vivienne Tam, a womenswear label based in New York. A year later, she completed a BFA degree in fashion, with a plan to move permanently to New York right after graduation.

There was just one catch; the year was 2008, smack in the middle of the Great Recession, when the global economy pushed unemployment to record highs. Entry-level jobs were more competitive than ever. Eleanor didn't know many people in the New York fashion industry, other than the few she'd met the summer before. Among the few was

Diego, who worked in public relations at Tommy Hilfiger. Diego was smart, funny, kind. Maybe he'd have a few ideas.

Eleanor wrote him a text. She'd be up there looking for an apartment soon, and did he want to grab coffee? She sent the message and said a little prayer. Maybe her great-grandfather's Big Favorite button still held some magic.

THE MYSTERY AND MYTH OF "SELF-MADE"

Eleanor needed help to open the gates of Oz. Just as Dorothy had her ruby slippers, Eleanor held a fashion degree and a belief that entrepreneurship lived in her bones, but she needed more.

She needed allies.

By *allies*, we don't necessarily mean friends, although many of your alliances may blossom into lasting friendships. If you're a student, your allies are professors, classmates, alumni, staff members with whom you come into contact. After college, allies are your colleagues and acquaintances. Your boss is an ally. The person you know from pickleball is a potential ally, too. **Allies share information, swap favors, make introductions, hire each other, and promote one another's projects on social media.**

And yet, so many aspiring entrepreneurs fail to see the need for allies. We've all succumbed to the fantasy that the most brilliant businesspersons must have done it all on their own. "The myth of the self-made man is at the core of the American Dream," writes researcher Aaron Duncan.

After all, who doesn't love a good bootstraps story? The online bookseller who eventually funds his own private space exploration company to become one of the world's first citizen astronauts.

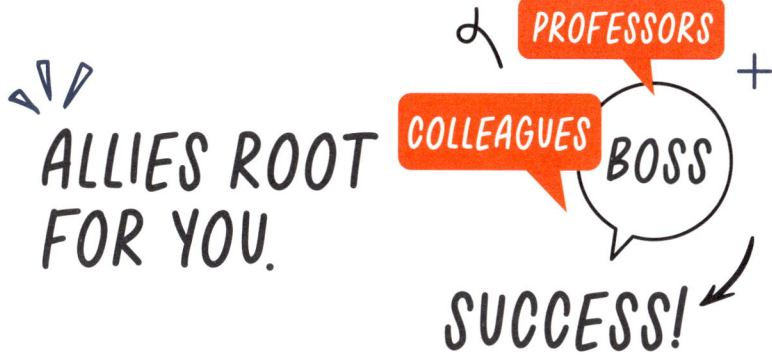

The girl raised in the rural South without electricity or running water, now widely regarded as the world's most recognizable TV personality. The fatherless young man who became one of history's greatest baseball stars. Each of these highly successful people — Bezos, Oprah, and A-Rod, respectively — seem to have risen to global fame on the strength of their talent alone, but where would Bezos be without Shel Kaphan, the man who wrote the company's first line of code? Where would Oprah be without Dennis Swanson, who took a risk on an unknown talent and hired her for her first daytime show? And how about A-Rod? More on him later on.

THE GLOW-UP

Diego, much to Eleanor's relief, enthusiastically agreed to coffee. A few days later, she flew to the city, anxious for his advice about where she might work.

"What are you looking for?" Diego asked.

"Anything," Eleanor said, smiling.

He told her that Tommy Hilfiger needed someone who could help manage editorial shoots and gown loans.

"It sounds amazing," she said.

"There's a catch," he said.

Her office would have to be a windowless sample closet: humble beginnings for a graduate from an elite university. But so what? This was a closet at one of the great American fashion houses, in a building on Madison Avenue. As soon as she was back home, she sent in her portfolio and résumé and the job was hers.

> **"I was mesmerized by the magic of fashion—**
> **I didn't care what I was doing; I just wanted to be**
> **in the industry."**

She got to work tagging gowns for red carpet events and *Vogue* photoshoots. It was exhausting and exhilarating work. She showed up early, stayed late, remembered names, got noticed. After just six months in the windowless closet, Eleanor's boss made her a dream offer: the company was relaunching a new line and they wanted to promote her. Her fashion dreams were coming true.

"I became a familiar face to Tommy Hilfiger himself," she said.

Research confirms what Eleanor observed first-hand: allies give your career a serious glow-up. They help you to get unstuck, inspired, and hired. Career coach Matt Youngquist explains that 70–80% of jobs are neither published nor advertised — and yet those jobs get filled. How do candidates find out about those open positions? They know somebody. Why bother sifting through an endless digital blur of applications and LinkedIn profiles when a trusted ally throws a good name your way? Allies rarely make bad recommendations. According to LinkedIn, "People who are referred for a job are a whopping nine times more likely to get it."

PEOPLE WHO ARE REFERRED FOR A JOB ARE 9X MORE LIKELY TO GET IT

Plus, according to a recent study in *The Journal of Applied Psychology*, allies don't merely help you get hired; they also directly correlate to earning a higher salary, as well as increased lifelong career satisfaction.

All this talk about who-you-know can smack of elitism. And it can feel unfair: some are born in the right place to the right people with the right names and fall headlong into the right opportunities. Others, not so much, due to social inequity, systemic racism, economic disparity, and other circumstances. LinkedIn CEO Jeff Weiner calls this challenge the network gap. **You can close that gap with allies.** Studies show that those who've been historically marginalized in their professions, including women and BIPOC employees, benefit exponentially from cultivating a wider group of allies in their careers.

After a year in New York, Eleanor's own group of allies had grown beyond all expectation. There was Diego, of course, and her colleagues at Tommy Hilfiger, not to mention the professors who opened her eyes to the wonders of fashion, the college advisers who helped her understand the value of internships and networking. Each relationship helped propel her career forward. She'd been out of college hardly twelve months and had already traveled the world for work and met many of her heroes. The world was hers, and she was just getting started. **Where would she go next?**

BE THE ALLY EVERYONE WANTS TO WORK WITH

After two years at Tommy Hilfiger, she left to work for Tory Burch, a new star in high-end American fashion whose eponymous label had taken off after an on-air endorsement by Oprah in its first year. In her first year as a knitwear designer for the company, Eleanor learned a lot about growing a young brand.

"When the company is yours, every decision matters," she said. "Where to locate, who to work with, packaging. Every decision costs money."

Everywhere she worked, Eleanor made an impression. Remembering Diego's kindness to her, she observed, listened, and offered a hand to anyone she could. Her success at Tory Burch led her to another gig in knitwear design two years later at J.Crew. She got to work directly with legendary CEO Mickey Drexler, the leader who'd transformed J.Crew into a global fashion behemoth of upscale prepwear.

After seven years in the industry, Eleanor had worked with some of the biggest fashion houses and designers in the US. At Tommy Hilfiger, she learned the centrality of runway shows to sales and marketing strategies. At Tory Burch, she learned how to form strong alliances with wholesalers. At J.Crew, she learned about scale. She was ready to start her own company. She started inviting new allies for drinks — startup veterans, people who knew angel investors.

 She had an idea. Office attire for women was tragically boring: she could elevate office workwear!

Her grandfather had innovated workwear for laborers and farmworkers. Why couldn't she do the same for professional women?

Eleanor partnered with friend and ally Sali Christeson and founded Argent, a womenswear brand focused on elevating women's office attire while helping reduce work-related microaggressions (hello, functional pockets!). Eleanor's conscientious, thoughtful designs scored four patents, were featured everywhere from *Vogue* and *Glamour* to *New York* magazine, and found a celebrity clientele, including Hillary Clinton and Gloria Steinem. Forbes named her on a list of "upstart entrepreneurs redefining the American dream," and Eleanor started forming even more ambitious plans.

HOW TO BUILD YOUR OWN ARMY OF ALLIES

Eleanor built her network by embodying designer Derek Blasberg's dictum: happy to be here, easy to work with. Sounds simple, though it's anything but. This means you need to be curious and hardworking, a playful problem-solver and serious about results. But above all else, you must be present. Those who are available (and make time for others) get remembered.

Today, most Gen Z students and young professionals overwhelmingly prefer more abstracted modes of communication — texts over phone calls, email over Zoom, Zoom over in-person meetings — and for good reason. These technologies save time and money. In the first year of the pandemic, thanks to not commuting into the office, the average American worker gained nearly nine days in a calendar year. Nine free days to do with what you like! No wonder so many of us love the idea of remote work.

We gained time, but lost connections and allies. The nuances and shades of meaning that draw us into alliances with like-minded persons — say, through eye contact, body language, the tone of a greeting — cannot yet be duplicated via text, meme, or DM. Even Zoom has its limitations.

GET OUT THERE!

Studies show that in-person interactions build stronger, more meaningful relationships, professionally and socially. Remote work may be here to stay, but the surest way to build the strongest alliances is in person.

Every student and young professional can find plenty of formal networking opportunities — career fairs, recruiter presentations, conferences, etc. — but don't limit yourself to official networking functions. Consider places you already interact with others: class, the yoga studio, the dorm, the grocery store, your favorite café. At work, bend a colleague's ear for feedback on a project. If you're a student, on the first day of class, stick around and introduce yourself to the professor. They'll remember you the next time you need something: advice, a deadline extension, a recommendation letter, an introduction.

The best alliances happen organically. They're not forced. Find kindred spirits by saying yes more than no. If friends are heading out to dinner after class, even though you'd rather unwind with Netflix, shut your laptop and go. When colleagues nudge you to join them for cocktails, even though you'd rather zone out with your puppy on the couch, say yes. The puppy will still love you. These casual interactions expand your network in ways you can't yet foresee. You're not out there looking for your next best friend, necessarily. **You're out there to meet new people, learn what you don't know, and build connections that will bear fruit one day.** As the old proverb says, "If you want to go fast, go alone. If you want to go far, go together.""

THE MOST IMPORTANT ALLY

When we think of allies, we so often think of peers, classmates, and colleagues, other dreamers aspiring to launch their own startups, brands, and careers. And you'll need them. But don't stop there. **Look up, and you might just find the greatest ally of all: a mentor.**

When Alex was eleven years old, his parents divorced and his life was forever changed. He could have become embittered and jaded, skeptical of those in authority, especially the men, fearing they too might abandon him. In those days, what he loved most was baseball. After school in his hometown of Miami, Florida, he'd race to the Boys and Girls Club to play a pickup game with his big brothers. These games bolstered his confidence and helped him hone his skills. By high school, Alex could out swing and outthrow much more seasoned players, but without anyone to guide him, he lacked the confidence to push his game further. That was until Coach Rich Hofman sat him down after practice one day and told Alex that he could be great, but needed to work harder.

Alex wanted to shrug this off. He was already great! College scouts were already eyeing him. He'd been told he could play on the US Olympic team and might even get drafted. But Coach Hofman insisted on working with him in private — to strengthen his mental toughness alongside the physical.

> **"I realized then the power of fatherhood, mentorship, and a positive voice in my life,"** Alex said. **"And that made all the difference."**

In 1993, Alex turned pro. Today, we know him as A-Rod, the Yankee legend, MLB All-Star, American League MVP, and World Series Champion. He retired after twenty-two seasons and soon turned pro in entrepreneurship. Having experienced the transformative benefits of Coach Hofman's mentorship, Alex sought out business wisdom from those in his network, including Magic Johnson, legendary basketball player and investment tycoon, and Warren Buffett, the ninth richest man in the world. He planned regular meetings with Magic and annual chats with Warren, while sharing the business and investment advice he received with other professional athletes. All the while, he was amassing a real estate empire of over 14,000 multi-family properties in New York and Florida. Alex's diligent pursuit of allyship has paid dividends, and his extensive venture capital and real estate portfolios are worth an estimated $350 million.

Throw off fear and resistance and reach out to teachers, industry veterans, even family friends. Open your ears and your heart to what they have to say. After all, mentees are five times more likely to be promoted. Not to mention that a whopping **90% of professionals with a mentor report being happy in their careers.** The rewards of mentorship are many. Borrow a page from A-Rod's playbook and you may see a potential mentor right in front of you.

ELEANOR SCORES BIG

After a few years of success as cofounder of Argent, her first startup, Eleanor saw a new opportunity.

"I was at Walgreens and holding a six pack of novelty Valentine's Day underwear," she said. This is when she got her big idea. She'd been in the midst of packing for a business trip and needed clean underwear. "I went to the only store that was open and left with these hideous, polyester-blend, heart-covered underpants."

"I need to fix this," she thought.

She sketched out a solution: a sustainable brand devoted to natural materials, comfort, and recycling. It felt audacious, and absolutely necessary. She called her brand The Big Favorite, in honor of her family history. **She devoted the startup to reducing landfill waste by contributing to "a circular system that's better for this great big world."**

The Big Favorite's products — tanks, tees, briefs, and more — would utilize 100% pima cotton, eliminating plastic particles, and the company would offer a recycling option. Once the clothes have been loved and worn, customers could send them back to be upcycled back into new Big Favorite goods. No more throwaway Valentine undies. The Big Favorite would offer an "eco-friendly supply chain" from the bottom-up. "People care about the companies they support, and how those companies operate on a global scale," Eleanor said. "Consumers want quality, comfort, and style, and they also want to know that the places they shop are mindful of their impact on the planet." She launched in 2020 and instantly earned rave reviews from *Vogue*, *Marie Claire*, and *Fast Company*. In a few short years, The Big Favorite has already begun transforming the textile industry. Without Eleanor's many allies — investors, influencers, journalists, clients, celebrities, designers, colleagues, alumni friends, former professors, and her alma mater — the epic success of The Big Favorite would not have happened. Find your allies, and watch your startup dreams come true.

BE THE ALLY

"Building a company is like having a baby: you can't
go it alone. The world runs on relationships and
hard work—in that order."

— Eleanor Turner

**You need to convince people to dream the
same dream that you do.**

— Guy Kawasaki, chief evangelist of Canva

2

The Believer

Just a few years after graduating with a BFA in graphic design, India had already become one of the hottest hires in the Atlanta design scene. As a student, she completed internships across an array of industries, from Cartoon Network to Astral Brands, a beauty company. Even before graduation, she was offered a coveted position creating public health infographics for the CDC, headquartered in Atlanta. After a couple years at the CDC, she was lured away to Turner Sports, where she produced content for networks like Upwave. India spoke the language of visual communication like few could. Public health, professional sports — she could do it all. CNN got word of this young designer and soon offered India a new role, designing graphics for breaking news. She was on top of the world and still in her early twenties.

India loved the challenge of working with elite teams, but despite the adrenaline rush of headlines and breaking news, she found her heart aiming even higher. She wanted to use her design talents to change the world.

As a child in Durham, North Carolina, India grew up around strong women who held passionate beliefs and made those beliefs central to their careers. Her godmother founded the Southeast Regional Economic Justice Network and her mother, a founder of Youth for Social Changes, traveled internationally to champion the rights of the oppressed and disenfranchised. "I learned a lot from those women and felt I needed to continue that legacy in my career," India said. Her undergraduate education helped her see that all work needs a *why*. A great visual campaign must go deeper than the surface. "My professors placed great emphasis on intention in every project."

It's not just about how something looks. Who will be touched by this work? Why does this work matter?

India knew her work at CNN and the CDC mattered. She was devoting her talents to communicating important, world-changing, and life-saving information to viewers and readers — but something was missing.

One day she heard about a panel — cohosted by Goodie Nation, Habitat for Humanity, and the Atlanta BeltLine — with a focus on how to make the city more inclusive. India attended the panel and was profoundly inspired to see all the intellectual talent that was being focused on solving some of Atlanta's most pressing challenges. When the panel was over, **she introduced herself to the host and enthusiastically shared her story**, telling them how she had been volunteering at area shelters and was already designing résumés for women experiencing homelessness to help them find employment and economic independence.

"You should apply to our incubator," she remembers the host saying, and then going on to explain that he oversaw a program to provide space and mentoring to new startups.

India had an idea. As a volunteer, she had seen that many people experiencing homelessness had a more urgent challenge than finding employment: Before they could even apply for jobs or government benefits, they needed identification. Most unhoused people had no way of proving who they were. Obtaining a government ID can be a monumentally difficult task for someone with no home address, no birth certificate, no Social Security card, and little or no access to computers or transportation. Many of these Atlantans were at the bottom of a deep hole, and India wanted to use her design knowledge to lift them out. Throughout her career, she had learned a lot about **user experience design** (helping users navigate websites and apps) and **service design** (improving how users interact with physical and digital environments), and she knew she could use that knowledge to better navigate the bureaucratic nightmare of obtaining ID.

She didn't quite know how her nascent startup would solve this problem, but that had never intimidated her before. She would figure it out. She had all the design knowledge and passion she needed. She believed.

THE WORLD NEEDS YOU

Entrepreneurs are born believers who hold deeply personal ideas about how to make the world better. A belief in the magic of childhood led to the founding of toy company Mattel. Tom's of Maine, maker of toothpaste and other personal care products, was born out of two parents' search for healthy products for their children. A concern for internet privacy led to the founding of DuckDuckGo. India's own startup dreams evolved out of compassion for the dispossessed and displaced.

You, as well, may not yet be sure just how you want to change the world. **You've got time to work it out.** All of us are animated by a strong set of core beliefs; some are conscious, some are unconscious and waiting to emerge. These core beliefs drive our decisions, dreams, careers, and lives. The most successful students and entrepreneurs know what they care about and why, and they forge careers that allow them to communicate their beliefs and values through their work. You want to make a living — absolutely — and you want to make a difference, too.

After all, you're Gen Z. You want to use your creative brilliance and intellectual gifts to change the world. Nearly 94% of your generation wants companies to advance social and environmental causes, compared to 86% of the total population. And, nearly half of all Gen Z members aspire to devote their own professional talents to advocacy, just like India. Where previous generations promoted important causes largely through volunteerism and donations, Gen Z sees little distinction between advocacy and profession. According to entrepreneur Mark Perna, this generation wants a "workplace that will embrace and empower [their] inventive spirit."

What kind of world do you want to create? How might your mind and heart work together to build that world? Maybe you're passionate about the progress afforded by technology — solar power, food access, health equity. Maybe you're devoted to literacy or the creative empowerment of rural or urban communities. Maybe you want to educate schoolchildren about the joys and benefits of farming, homesteading, and nature. Maybe you aspire to rid the world of human trafficking or champion political action on climate change.

 **What matters is that you start thinking now about your why.**

The purpose and passion of youth can become the profession of a lifetime. Just look at the story of entrepreneur Yvon Chouinard, a believer for the ages.

WHY YOU CLIMB

The year was 1957 when Yvon Chouinard, an American of French-Canadian descent, went to a local junkyard and purchased a used coal-fired forge. The products from this forge would be the start of a multibillion-dollar company. Chouinard's drive started from the convergence of idealism and annoyance. Many climbers of the era still used iron pitons, which pierced the granite to be used as an anchor and could not be removed — wounds in the rock that did not align with the ideals of Chouinard's naturalist heroes, Thoreau, Emerson, and Muir. Why were climbers still using these destructive little tools?

So, Chouinard began creating his own pitons of chrome steel, which could be removed and reused later. Word of the revolutionary pitons spread, and soon Chouinard's passionate hobby became a fledgling business. By the 1970s demand for his products had increased, and he had met and married his wife, Malinda. As the company expanded Yvon and Malinda Chouinard turned their attention to other needs in their community of climbers, surfers, and backpackers, and in 1973, Patagonia was born. It would go on to become the **most conscientious (and most successful)** adventure-gear retailer in the world.

Across the fifty years since its founding, Patagonia has revolutionized ecofriendly manufacturing processes, being one of the first companies to use organic, pesticide-free cotton and ethically sourced wool and goose down. Where other brands turn a blind eye to poor labor conditions, Patagonia assumed additional manufacturing costs to reform their Taiwanese workrooms, becoming California's first B Corp, a certification given to companies observing rigorous environmental and labor standards. While competitors looked only at profit margins, Chouinard built a culture around informed processes, treating production and product with equal weight.

Environmentalism is not a marketing angle for Chouinard's company. It's the very reason for its existence. He has proven that devotion to a cause is not a hindrance to the bottom line, but rather a boon. Today, Patagonia is worth $3 billion, with manufacturing facilities in fifteen nations and stores on five continents.

In a longitudinal study, Isaac Getz and Laurent Marbacher, cofounders of the Altruistic Enterprise Institute, learned that companies like Patagonia are financially successful through prioritizing social value alongside economic value. **When a company stands for something — in word and action — customers notice.**

These days, Chouinard, now in his eighties, prefers to spend his summers teaching the art of tenkara fly fishing to future anglers or petitioning to preserve the southernmost region of Chile — the source of the Patagonia name — among other causes. "The capitalist ideal is you grow a company and focus on making it as profitable as possible," he said. "Then, when you cash out, you become a philanthropist." Instead, Chouinard believes "a company has a responsibility to do that all along — for the sake of the employees, for the sake of the planet."

TIME TO FLY

In those early months at the incubator, India worked hard with singular focus. Like a superhero, she had a respectable day job, designing infographics for the CNN Breaking News and Interactives Team, but by night she fought injustice. Her product in this fight would be new software to reduce homelessness by helping dispossessed Atlantans obtain identification and start rising out of poverty. Her clients would be the shelters and other nonprofits around the city — because without an ID, their unhoused clients cannot get access to Medicaid, SNAP benefits (Supplemental Nutrition Assistance Program), library cards (to access computers and apply for employment), and more. Through her research, India knew these nonprofits would happily invest in the service Mini City provided.

India applied her knowledge of user experience design, service design, and visual communication — and she found allies who could code. After a year working on the problem, they developed software that successfully interfaces with state and federal databases to help clients obtain birth certificates — the single most essential step in the process of obtaining ID. Their product was, in the language of venture capital, an SaaS (Software as a Service). In addition to software, her team developed wristbands using NFC tech (near-field communication technology), each one about the size of an Apple Watch. These wristbands, available exclusively to unhoused people, allowed wearers to access Mini City tablet-based kiosks, set up around the city, which had begun to grow in number, from one in 2017 to more than twenty by 2023.

These technologies are projected to save cities millions of dollars in annual resources because access to support services is key to ending the cycle of poverty in which so many are trapped.

"If we can prove who you are, we can help you get what you need."

Before Mini City's appearance on the scene, unhoused people might wait up to a full calendar year to obtain identification — meaning a year without employment, income, or healthcare. Mini City's software reduces that time to mere days. **Tragedy became triumph.**

In early 2020, some four years after its creation, demand for Mini City's services began to grow by orders of magnitude. News of COVID-19 began to appear in the US, and shelters were already filling to capacity. The unhoused community of Atlanta would soon find itself in desperate need of more relief than ever.

India knew it was time to choose: CNN or Mini City. She didn't want to leave the news network. The pandemic was the biggest news story in a generation, and she knew her work could make an impact — but she felt something even stronger for Mini City. The need was too important to ignore, and with hope and courage, India gave her two weeks' notice at CNN. **Mini City had been a dream once. Now it was a career.**

KNOW THYSELF

Articulating your point of view is crucial to entrepreneurial success, says author Simon Sinek. Explaining his "Golden Circle" principle, Sinek says that while most people and companies understand the *what* and *how* of their job, very few understand their *why*.

This, argues Sinek, matters on a biological level. Our brains work from the inside out, with intangible emotion inspiring tangible actions. While mediocre companies pitch the flashy features of their product, expecting customers to reach for their wallets, brands like Apple and Patagonia **invite people into their story**, engaging them in a passionate conversation about their mission. People don't buy what you do, says Sinek. People buy why you do it.

You do not buy Apple products because they produce a unique product. Dozens of companies make products similar to the Mac-Book and iPhone, and much more affordably. No, you become an Apple customer because you're sold on their belief in marrying aesthetic beauty with user-friendly experience. Apple makes machines that don't feel like machines. There's a *why* there. Steve Jobs made computers beautiful and fun.

In the 1950s, legendary journalist Edward R. Murrow hosted a popular, five-minute segment on CBS Radio with the title: "This I Believe." Later adapted by NPR, inspiring a new generation of business leaders and believers, the segment features celebrities and others sharing a personal story that evinces their core beliefs. Check out their website for some of our favorites, including essays by food writer Jason Sheehan (about his belief in the healing power of food), skateboarding legend Tony Hawk (about taking pride in your profession), and Ashleigh, a student (who writes about her own entrepreneurial journey). Try writing your own, "This I believe" statement, no more than 500 words or so. **You'll know more about yourself when you're finished than when you began.**

Or try this: Write down a list of your top twenty-five beliefs about the world, i.e., what's most important in your life, your future or current profession, your family. Make each one a complete sentence, starting with "I believe." *I believe in freedom of expression. I believe the world should laugh more. I believe reading can change your life. I believe everyone deserves healthcare. I believe coding can give you purpose.* Take time writing out these statements. Be funny, be earnest, be wild, be bold, be honest. **Let yourself shine through.** Show nobody if it suits you.

Circle the five beliefs that truly speak to you and cross out the other twenty. This doesn't mean you don't really believe these statements — you do! This just means those five are the biggies. Those are the ones that will likely shape your career and your life. Spanish philosopher José Ortega y Gasset said, "Tell me to what you pay attention, and I will tell you who you are."

TO THE MOON AND BACK

A year after leaving CNN to work full time as CEO of her own startup, India and her small team at Mini City were thriving, growing faster than anyone could have anticipated. They had built innovative software, helped countless clients obtain government ID, installed nineteen kiosks around the city, and trained over one hundred caseworkers with the Mini City software to assist Atlanta's unhoused community. What they needed now was funding, an investment that would help them scale up and **keep growing**.

India applied for and was awarded funding from her alma mater through SCADpro Fund, an investment initiative developed exclusively for alumni of the Savannah College of Art and Design. The university provided resources, space, mentoring, and funding. This afforded India and her team more time to refine their product, polish their pitch, and perfect their business plan.

SKILLS AND ABILITIES
what do you like to do?

PERSONALITY TRAITS
how do you really work?

FIND YOUR
WHY

BELIEFS
what does a more perfect
world look like?

DREAMS
what do you want out of
life, now and later?

USE YOUR NOTES TO DRAFT
A SHORT ESSAY. AT THE TOP, WRITE

"THIS I BELIEVE."

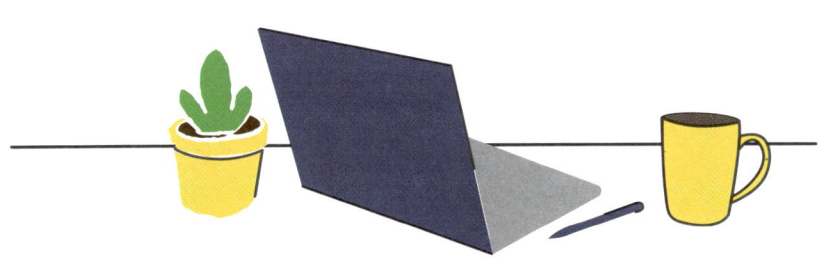

India knew that if she wanted to grow, she needed to think beyond Atlanta. How could she help the estimated 500,000 unhoused people across the country? India's past success and the audacity of her bold new vision led to an invitation to participate in a roundtable with one of the world's most influential business leaders: Sundar Pichai, CEO of Alphabet, parent company of Google. Funding from Google would take Mini City to the next level as a profitable, national company helping to eradicate homelessness.

India was one of four founders invited to pitch to the Google leader, and she was understandably nervous. The other three young entrepreneurs were working on projects related to cancer detection and AI-driven sign language translation. India suddenly felt very insignificant. What could she contribute to the conversation with this Silicon Valley legend? She would be laughed out of the room. She couldn't compete with cancer research and artificial intelligence. During the roundtable, where she explained her passion to help the unhoused and how this passion inspired the tech, Sundar lit up. "This is a daunting problem," India recalls him saying, "How did you solve it? It just seems so impossible!"

He was impressed, and India was relieved and happy.

After the meeting, she got a message from Google. They wanted to invest, promising $100,00 in funding — Mini City would be included in the Black Founders Fund portfolio! Six years since first conceiving of her company and just over a year since leaving CNN to work fulltime at Mini City, India had everything she had ever dreamed of: a financially successful company leveraging design thinking to solve an urgent social problem. These days, she spends her time innovating and dreaming up new ways to apply design and technology to improve the lives of the most vulnerable. India challenges her team, clients, and investors to **live the life of a believer** — to find their why.

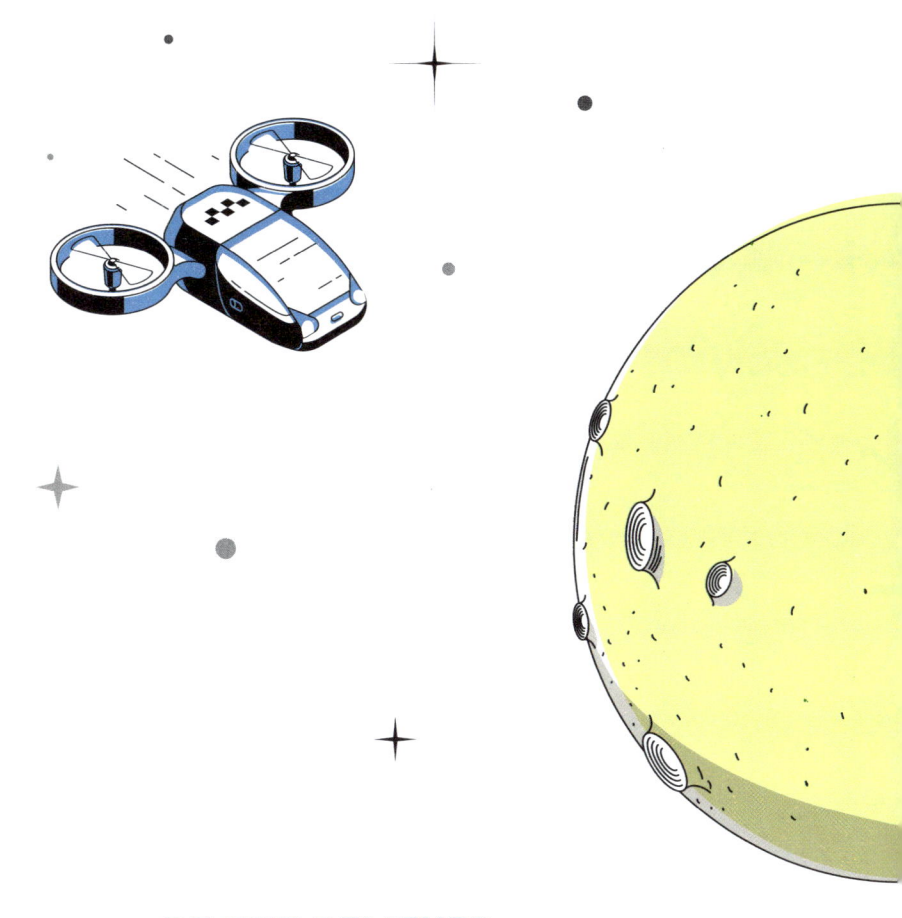

BE THE BELIEVER

"Maybe you want to put a computer in every home
in America or help every child fly to the moon;
you can make the world what you want it to be,
if you believe."

— India Jha

Do not follow where the path may lead, but go where there is no path, and leave a trail.

—adapted from "Wind-Wafted Wild Flowers" by Muriel Strode.

3

The Hacker

reamers dream up new inventions in the unlikeliest of places. Interface designer Greg Christie invented the swipe to unlock iPhone feature while observing the sliding lock mechanism on bathroom doors. Electronics giant Nokia was dreamt up in a Finnish paper mill. One of the wildest entrepreneurial success stories in recent years — making waves from TikTok to ESPN — was danced into existence in a baseball stadium in a small Southern town. The city is Savannah, Georgia, and the story is bananas.

It all started a few years ago, when Jesse Cole was named general manager of a failing baseball team in North Carolina. Cole had his work cut out for him. How could he get fans in the seats? Baseball alone could not swing it.

Describing his "aha" moment for the *New York Times*, Cole said he first tried the usual "zany promotions" — free giveaways and T-shirt cannons — but then one day, he realized he didn't need to add more fun off the field. He needed to add more fun on the field. Inspired, Cole convinced a few players to stage a dance in between innings.

"Though some team members balked when asked to learn choreography, a core crew started performing simple routines between innings," writes Margaret Fuhrer in the *Times*. One night during a game, Cole caught a glimpse of a couple in the middle of a conversation when the wife interrupted her husband.

"Shut up, honey," she said, "they're about to dance!'"

"That's when I was like, all right, we've got something here," said Cole.

Soon after, Cole and his wife Emily decided to start a new team that would fully embrace their philosophy of fun. They found the perfect opportunity in Savannah, where the historic Grayson Stadium sat idle and empty. The team would be called the Savannah Bananas, a ridiculous name for a team ready to put on a ridiculous show, and in the process create baseball games that nobody wanted to leave early. The Bananas joined the Coastal Plain League, a summer league of college players with MLB ambitions. In a short time, the team started turning heads and going viral over and over. Why? Well, here's just a few from many reasons: they sometimes play in kilts; the coaches dance in between pitches; and their dance team, the "Banana Nanas," is comprised exclusively of grandmothers. Some games even feature "Banana Ball," a condensed baseball-like game with even zanier antics — think pitchers on stilts. Banana Ball would prove so popular, in fact, that Cole would eventually dedicate the entire franchise to it.

> **It's baseball, but it's also part circus and part professional wrestling, with cruise-like entertainment and Harlem Globetrotter sensibilities.** —ESPN

The initial magic of Cole's Innovation was that, despite the wild fun, the Bananas still play baseball. A recent study showed how their players had an improved "batting average, on-base percentage and slugging percentage," when they played with the Bananas, compared to playing on their college teams back home. They've won the Coastal Plain League title three times from 2016 to 2022, and no fewer than eleven current or past Bananas players were signed in the 2022 MLB draft. More amazing still, the stadium was packed for every game — all 4,000 seats — **with 50,000 fans on the waitlist**.

Jesse Cole is many things: an enthusiastic team owner, a viral marketing guru, a showbiz wiz in a bright yellow tuxedo. But what he truly is, and what all entrepreneurs are, at heart, is a hacker.

THE MAGIC OF THE HACK

Hackers aren't just computer programmers. They exist across sectors, from healthcare and hospitality to finance and filmmaking, and challenge outmoded conventions in pursuit of breakthrough results and economic value. The one quality you find in every hacker, however, is their outsider status.

"Big innovation most often happens when an outsider who may be far away from the surface of the problem reframes the problem in a way that unlocks the solution," says Dr. Karim Lakhani. "When individuals are given the opportunity to apply their unique insight to a problem, they can solve it."

In the multibillion-dollar world of professional sports, Jesse Cole was an outsider with no experience on the national stage. He'd never played pro sports and never worked in sports marketing. As an outsider, he wasn't burdened by tradition, and was thus free to see beyond the strictures of others. To sell tickets and fill seats, he didn't look to successful pro clubs: he looked to Walt Disney and P. T. Barnum.

"I didn't want to learn from the baseball industry," Cole told the *New York Times*. "I wanted to learn from the greatest entertainers out there." He created one of the most successful startups in recent sports history because he hacked his way to a solution, finding his answer where nobody else was looking.

CURIOSITY!

Hackers' strength lies in their curiosity: where others see unbreakable rules, hackers see possibility.

Most airlines cater to passengers in first class.

What if you created an affordable airline that focused on everyone else?

No business class tickets, no priority seating, no baggage fees, and less formality? Herb Kelleher asked these questions in launching Southwest Airlines, the world's largest low-cost airline.

In the automotive industry, purchasing a used car has always presented an irksome process for seller and buyer: limited stock, limited seller knowledge, price-points that vary wildly (depending on where you live), having to argue over deals at a used car lot, and other annoyances.

What if you brought the car to the customer, free of haggling?

The answer is Carvana, the fastest-growing car dealer in the US and one of the youngest companies to make the Fortune 500 list.

What if grocery stores devoted less time to neatly stacked goods and more to affordable products? That's Aldi. What if, instead of preparing food back in the kitchen, you let customers watch you make their meal and be able to tell you exactly how they want it made? That's Subway. What if you solved the honeybee decline, not with traditional conservation measures, but with something altogether unexpected?

THE HACKER SHE WAS BORN TO *bee*

"Remember, fifty concepts are due next Tuesday," said the professor, over the din of zipping backpacks and shuffling feet.
"Fifty?" thought Anna, "I better start tonight."

A newly declared industrial design major, Anna was eager to dive into her first assignment: create a self-sufficient object that stimulated the growth of plants. She'd considered creating a pot that grows with the plant or an automated grow light, or maybe a wind-powered compost maker.

"Boring," she sighed.

As she rushed toward the doorway, her eyes honed in on spot of yellow and black on the sweatshirt in front of her: a miniature embroidered honeybee. Bees! Yes! Anna remembered *Vanishing of the Bees*, a documentary she'd watched a few years earlier, which shed ligh on the global diminution of bee populations. Her concept, she decided in that instant, should address the devastation of these crucial pollinators.

Once back in her dorm, Anna began her **research**. Bees, she learned, pollinate more than 80% of Europe's wildflowers. Their worldwide efforts mean one-third of every meal on the planet comes from plants pollinated by bees. Profitable global crops like almonds rely exclusively on bees for pollination and, without their assistance, biodiversity and world economies would dry up within a matter of years. And of course, the bee was her school's mascot, too.

Anna's brain was abuzz with ideas. She pulled out her sketchpad and began to draw concepts. Sketching helped her to wrap her mind around a tiny machine that could pollinate plants and flowers like an actual member of *Apis mellifera*. She drew one, then two, then over fifty concepts. At the next critique, one of Anna's models received high praise from her classmates and professor — her design for a tiny, self-pollinating drone.

"That's the one! You're onto something here," one classmate said.

"Make it look like a bee," suggested another.

"Paint it black and yellow."

"You could call it **Plan Bee**!" the professor said.

Anna expanded on her Plan Bee concept the following quarter by creating a 3D model of the drone, which earned her a silver medal for Environmental Design Preservation at the International Design Awards in Europe. Word of the revolutionary aerial pollinator soon spread to *Teen Vogue*, *Time*, and CNN, all of whom wanted to shine a light on this hopeful invention. Before she turned the tassel on her graduation cap, *Forbes* called. They wanted to see Plan Bee fly at their AgTech

Summit in California that summer. After a live demo, industry elites and investors swarmed her.

Like all great hackers, Anna **asked a question nobody else had**. While agribusiness focused exclusively on how to grow bee colonies — a noble task, to be sure — Anna asked: What if we can replicate the work of bees with good design? This is how Anna's first startup was born. It would not be her last.

MEDITATION MEETS TRIANGULATION

Hacking begins with mindfulness: a nonjudgmental state of awareness in which ideas flow freely and the inner eye roves far and wide across intellectual terrain, somewhere between brainstorming and daydreaming. Most of us find mindfulness so difficult because the harried busyness of everyday life compels us to pay attention only to our most urgent tasks — where to be, when to leave, how to dress. Intentional mindfulness frees you, for five minutes or five hours, from those demands and lets the mind run free.

To become more mindful (and access the hacker within), find ways to engage your body and five senses with yoga, dance, Pilates, swimming laps, a short run, or even a thirty-minute walk. A recent study that tasked participants with completing "mental tasks that required imagination" found that 100% of those participating "produced more creative ideas while walking, as compared to sitting." Walking has long been a favorite practice of novelists and philosophers, helping generate new ideas when stories and thoughts grow stale. The study also found that "when those who had walked sat down afterward, the creativity boost lingered — great news for anyone who takes walking breaks and then returns to a desk."

Once you've made time for mindfulness, try your hand at triangulation: the application of multiple perspectives onto a single question or challenge, frequently including approaches from an altogether different field. Consider how Jesse Cole applied the thinking of great entertainers (rather than pro sports managers and owners) to enliven baseball games. Scientist Stephon Alexander used triangulation to

apply ideas from the work of jazz musician John Coltrane to create new theories in the field of physics. When Candace Nelson was pregnant with her first child and couldn't quell her late-night sugar cravings, she immediately thought of the convenience of ATMs, a 24/7 financial service. Triangulating the two very different industries — food-service and finance — she conceived of the Sprinkles Cupcake ATM, which served freshly baked cupcakes to shoppers at all hours of day and night.

Successful triangulation requires you to be **informed about the world**, as when Anna's memory of a documentary film inspired her award-winning, attention-getting startup. This same gift for triangulation led Anna to reframe declining bee populations, not as an agricultural challenge, but a technological one. All she had to do now was launch the business.

ATTACK OF THE MUMMIES

After Anna's big debut at the Forbes AgTech Summit, just weeks after graduation and in the midst of dozens of media interviews, she turned her attention to transforming the Plan Bee prototype into a scalable, sellable product. What she lacked in agribusiness experience she made up for with a passion for problem-solving.

"You're not going to know everything right off the bat and you're not going to be an expert in all areas of that space," said Anna.

First, she needed to do some field-testing. With her prototype in hand, Anna headed to Australia to assess Plan Bee's pollination prowess among the almond fields down under. The drone flew valiantly, but navigating the orchards' hilly terrain and branch-filled groves proved highly problematic for the tiny flying machine.

"It just didn't work," Anna said. Even though the drone could fit in a human hand, the device was still too large, the tight spaces for pollinating too narrow.

"Well, where can I go from here?" she wondered.

She could've given up and walked away, but her design education imparted to her the need for revision and iteration in the face of feedback. She loved the almond farmers she'd met in Australia, and after heading back to the US, she paid a visit to Mel Machado, Vice President of Member Relations for Blue Diamond, one of the world's top almond producers, for the inside scoop on his needs.

Pollination, it turned out, was not his main problem. He brought in truckloads of live bees for that. He had an altogether new challenge in growing his almonds. "If you have a solution to the navel orangeworm crisis, I am all ears," she remembers Machado saying over lunch.

"Tell me more," Anna replied. She loved a good challenge. Navel orangeworms, Machado explained, can inflict epic destruction on almond crops, where they burrow into almond nuts still left on trees after the harvest (known as "mummies") and lay waste to groves each spring when they emerge as moths. This can cost farmers as much as $1,700 per acre and diminish crops by close to 20%. The only existing solutions to the problem were costly and ineffective: violently shaking each tree to release the mummies, which harms the plant, or removing them by hand.

A good hacker knows when to move on. Anna's experience with Plan Bee showed her that flying a tiny robot through the byzantine maze of branches was not feasible. She had to say goodbye to the honeybee drone and devise an entirely new solution. "With prototype development, **when something doesn't work, it doesn't surprise me**," she said. "That's part of the process."

She needed to pivot to a ground assault. Her company would not pollinate almonds in spring. In the winter, they would remove navel orangeworm-infested mummies.

Anna named her new company InsightTRAC. Working with a small team over the next few years, she developed a solution: a mobile robot — roughly the size of a riding lawnmower — which seeks out mummies and uses proprietary technology to knock them to the ground. This rover, topped with multiple turrets, uses machine learning to make its way through the grove, identifying mummies along the way with patented sight-tracking technology that creates a 3D map of each tree. Once spotted, the rover fires small biodegradable pellets at diseased mummies with surprising accuracy, dropping them to the earth, where workers quickly eliminate the pests long before they can cause any damage. Each rover is painted bright orange — in homage to its nemesis — and operates day and night, in rain or shine, to protect crops. The sound of the firing is not unlike a paintball gun: a faint pop.

After five years of prototyping, research, testing, and revision, InsightTRAC has gone on to revolutionize the almond industry, earning Indiana's Innovative Small Business of the Year Award in 2021, a Top Ten New Product Award at the 2022 World Ag Expo, and a Top 50 Innovation Award from Robotics Business Review. Anna now has a career she could have never imagined: she is the CEO of an award-winning company, which has grown to fifteen employees — industrial designers, electronics and software engineers, and more — and it all began with a college assignment.

Her design education, she said, gave her the tools to become an entrepreneur: **"You can either be comfortable, or you can step outside of your comfort zone and gain a whole new portfolio of experiences that you never would have had."** As a born hacker, she was once an outsider. Today, she's right in the middle of the action. "It's nuts!" she exclaimed.

BE THE HACKER

"You can either be comfortable, or you can step outside of your comfort zone and gain a whole new portfolio of experiences that you never would have had."

— Anna Haldewang

OPPORTUNITY ZONE

**Determine that the thing can and shall be done,
and then we shall find the way.**

— Abraham Lincoln

4

The Warrior

Quintin grew up in rural Elko, Georgia, where he worked on his grandfather's farm and dreamed of a life in the NBA. He knew this wildly distant ambition would demand strenuous work — only about one out of every 50,000 high school athletes ever set foot on a professional basketball court — but if raising and feeding cattle and hogs taught him anything, it was how to push past his own resistance to get the job done. When his grandfather gave him a task, he had to complete it.

"No ifs, ands, or buts about it," he said.

After his chores and homework were finished, "Q" (as he has been known from a young age) played ball for hours — by himself or with his cousins. His great idol was Michael Jordan of the Chicago Bulls, one of the greatest athletes in sports history, a warrior at heart who notoriously worked harder and put in more reps than his opponents. Q never forgot the moment in fourth grade when one of his classmates showed up to school in a new pair of Air Jordan XIV's. The shoe felt like a reflection of the player himself: powerful, elegant, attention-getting. Q couldn't get enough of his favorite athlete, devoting countless hours to watching Jordan play: "I admired his passion and drive for the game, his will to be the greatest ever."

Q had another love as fierce as his devotion to basketball: drawing. He especially loved sketching cars, sneakers, and characters from anime. His parents encouraged him to keep drawing and see where it would lead. Their support, coupled with his own talent and passion, made Q feel like he could do anything he wanted to.

Near the end of high school, like so many other aspiring young athletes, Q looked in the mirror and realized he would not be the next

Michael Jordan. But that didn't mean his dream of working in the NBA was over. **Like every great warrior, he knew he could find a way.** "I decided to focus on my skills as a designer," he said.

On a visit to SCAD, he learned about a major he'd never heard of before, industrial design, and saw that students had recently designed a functioning sportscar prototype. "I instantly knew that it was the place where I needed to be." He loved the "problem-solving required of automotive design, the necessity of superb drafting skills to create a beautiful product." His competitive spirit awoke once again. He got his portfolio together, applied, and was accepted.

Q's design professors invited him to try his hand, literally, at designing just about any product he could dream up. Soon he found himself drawing sneakers again, as he had in his younger days. He obsessively drew Jordans and new iterations of other basketball shoes. His classes gave him the design language to riff, to experiment, to try new contours and colorways. Q loved drawing shoes, which, as he told VoyageLA, "bridged [his] love for the lines of car design and the performance of basketball sneakers."

Sneaker design became his new dream. His sophomore year, he applied for an apprenticeship with Reebok, but was rejected. The footwear industry proved to be as competitive as basketball, but Q knew he had it in him to keep pushing. **Like all successful creative pros, he sketched out a plan**; one that would eventually take him across the country, across oceans, and all the way to the NBA.

WHAT EVERY WARRIOR NEEDS

Inside every entrepreneur is a joyful, focused warrior with an undefeatable spirit, animated by grit and passion. Warriors are champions — of themselves and others — who do not dwell on failure and instead focus on past successes and future outcomes. They devise a plan, enliven the plan with purpose and passion, and never look back.

Success at every stage of life and work demands dauntless optimism in the face of challenges. When we look at our heroes and idols, their triumphs appear inevitable and fated by the gods, when in fact, the most admired success stories include innumerable obstacles and setbacks. Warriors possess many special qualities, such as intelligence, natural talent, and a network of support, but there's one virtue above all others, available to anyone, that most often ensures victory. **It's a little word that possesses mighty power. It's called GRIT.**

Researcher Angela Duckworth, the world's foremost authority on the subject, defines grit as "passion and perseverance for long-term goals." She continues:

Grit isn't talent. Grit isn't luck. Grit isn't how intensely, for the moment, you want something. Instead, grit is about having what some researchers call an "ultimate concern" — a goal you care about so much that it organizes and gives meaning to almost everything you do.

One of the greatest predictors of grit, according to Duckworth, is education: "More educated adults were higher in grit than were less educated adults of equal age," she writes, based in findings from her landmark study. Earning a university degree, in particular, denotes a willingness to persist within and complete a designated, often rigorous, course of study. Without application, natural intelligence is useless.

Another marker of grit is conscientiousness, also known as diligence: the ability to complete a task with focused attention. Warriors understand the value of creative play, but they also know when to get serious. They discipline their heads, hands, and hearts with practice, iteration, rehearsal, endless hours in solitude: shooting hoops, writing scripts, creating and recreating sketch after sketch. Duckworth found that among young competitors in the Scripps National Spelling Bee, grit (measured in part by frequency of practice and preparation) was a better predictor of success than IQ.

Grit is a muscle that grows when you work it.

Warriors aren't born.

They're made.

THE SCRAPPY SNEAKERHEAD

Q could now clearly articulate his "ultimate concern." Though he didn't yet know if he wanted to work for one of his favorite brands, like Nike, or start his own line — that dream seemed almost too dreamy — he knew that he wanted to devote his talents to shoe design. He wanted **more than a job**. He wanted **a lifelong career** in the world of sneakers and shoes.

After his rejection for the Reebok apprenticeship, Q spent his junior year at university refining and selecting only the most superior work for his portfolio. He launched a new website featuring his designs and sketches, hoping to get noticed: the work paid off. The next summer, he landed an internship in Brooklyn with a small firm producing hiking boots for the European market.

"I gained so much knowledge on the process of making shoes and the logistics of what it takes to enter and finish production," he said. The experience energized him. Here he was, a young man from rural Georgia, living the creative life in the hippest borough of New York. Every day after work, when his friends would hit the city to explore, Q went straight back to his small apartment to work on his own designs and upload them to his website. He put in the reps, just like Jordan.

That summer, Q received an email from D'Wayne Edwards, former director for Nike's Jordan line, urging him to enter the PENSOLE contest. The winning design students would be invited to study in an intensive seminar with Edwards himself.

Q notes that he had learned "real world design experience" from his professors at SCAD, which helped him to understand that "when opportunities arise, you take them to gain more experience and build your network." (Remember Chapter 1? Your Professors are your allies!)

Q's continual devotion to improving his portfolio brought results. He was accepted! When his New York internship ended, he flew out to Portland to study with Edwards, one of his design heroes, at the PEN-SOLE Footwear Design Academy.

After his graduation from SCAD the following year, his old boss from Brooklyn called and asked if he'd be interested in working that summer in Dongguan, China, where their hiking boots were manufactured. Like a great athlete, Q wanted more moves in his playbook. He wanted to see how shoes got made. After a couple of months in Dongguan, working right there on the factory floor, he headed back to the States to take on the big brands back home.

Cue the training montage: Q, waking up before dawn to hone his craft, drawing, designing, creating more looks, expanding his design language. He entered dozens of shoe design competitions.

"I kept grinding," he said.

The grind paid off when Q won a national design competition for Power Force Apparel, which earned him serious attention. Job offers poured in. He knew if he joined an enormous team at one of the big brands — likely employing fifty or even one hundred designers — then he'd be at the bottom of a very crowded ladder. He didn't want to work for the giants. He wanted to defeat them.

 **"At this point in my career, I wanted to compete against the Goliaths of our industry."**

Power Force, the sponsoring company behind the competition that earned Q so much attention, offered him a job as their first in-house designer.

"Sign me up," he said.

It was at Power Force where Q saw a sneaker company built from the ground up, and he got to experience "a team of people pool together to complete one mission, one idea."

Next, Q worked for a Chinese brand as the lead designer at their LA studio. "I consciously chose this 'underdog' route because it still gave me a sense of competition against the bigger, American players," Q said. "It also provided the opportunity to expand my footwear experience internationally."

 After five years in the industry, Q felt he had enough knowledge to make his big move. He would call his company Q4 Sports, a clever play on his name and on the fourth quarter of a basketball game.

"That's where everything goes down to the wire. Win or lose. You get to see who wants it the most." Using his contacts, Q found an investment partner and he broke out on his own. It was time to ball.

EYE OF THE TIGER

Q's journey conjures the memory of another great warrior: Rocky Balboa, the fictional boxer famously portrayed by Sylvester Stallone. Balboa rises from obscurity on the mean streets of Philadelphia and conquers all obstacles on his way to defeating the world heavy weight champion, Apollo Creed. Stallone was the film's creative genius and he, like the character he was portraying, rose to the challenge: In the early 1970s, with just over $100 in his bank account, Stallone's screenplay generated serious Hollywood interest, and he wanted to play the lead role. He was offered $360,000 for the script — a stunning sum in those days — but the producers refused to give him the lead. Stallone, like Q, knew when to say no. Instead, the actor-writer raised his own funding and went on to produce and star in the film, earning nine Oscar nominations and two wins, including Best Picture. The film generated a total of eight spinoffs (including both the Rocky and Creed franchises), which have earned more than $790 million altogether.

Of course, **warriors aren't just athletes** — they come in many forms. Charles Schultz's drawings were rejected by his high school yearbook. Years later, his *Peanuts* comic strip became the greatest comic strip in the history of American newspapers, earning more than $1 billion annually from merchandising.

In the early 1990s, Jay-Z was turned down by every major record label in the business and he then formed his own label (Roc-A-Fella) to release his first album, selling CDs out of his car. Today he and his wife, Beyoncé, are worth an estimated $1.9 billion.

When Mary Kay Ash, a single parent, needed to earn income to provide for her three young children, she sought a career in sales. At the age of forty-five, after seeing men promoted over her despite her own impressive sales record, she invested her meager savings in a new company focused on beauty products for women. Today, Mary Kay Cosmetics is worth more than $3.25 billion.

After a lifetime of wayfaring professions — farmhand, streetcar conductor, life insurance salesman, and small-time restauranteur — Harland Sanders, who'd perfected his chicken recipe and preparation method late in life, opened the first Kentucky Fried Chicken franchise at the age of 62. KFC is now the second-largest fast-food franchise in the world.

How do you cultivate the grit necessary to become like these entrepreneurial warriors? Consider the facts: more than a third of entrepreneurs consider quitting before they even start; and of the two-thirds of startups and small businesses that launch, a whopping 50% fail within the first five years and 70% within the first ten years. Any entrepreneur's going to need to build strength and endurance long before they begin. Business author James Clear suggests three readymade tactics to build up your grit: articulate outcomes, work toward your desired outcomes every day, and push yourself into the unknown.

Follow Clear's suggestions and pretty soon, you'll find your capacity to endure, to endure and overcome has grown beyond all expectation.

WORK FOR *YOURS*

With the launch of Q4 Sports at the age of 26, Q faced his most daunting hurdle yet: convincing the world to wear his shoes. He sent samples to reviewers, influencers, and "wear-testers" who gave enthusiastic reviews. With his first line in production and prototypes in hand, he made the rounds. He called agents, front offices, back offices, any office with access to NBA players. These athletes needed shoes with performance and style, and Q's kicks had both.

Q approached players with a new proposal, very different from what the big sneaker brands offered. He wouldn't ask them to endorse a particular shoe with a cap on potential earnings, and athletes would have a bigger say in shoe design. "We're going to give you the ability to customize your own [sneaker] so that you can build your own brand," Q told them. "You're a true partner."

ARTICULATE OUTCOMES.

As we advocated in Chapter 2 ("The Believer"), entrepreneurs should verbalize—to allies, on social media, in a journal, on a vision board—what they want to achieve.

WORK TOWARD YOUR DESIRED OUTCOME EVERY DAY.

Devote one hour a day, outside of homework, to building your technical chops: sketching, writing, designing. Small goals lead to big ones: Duckworth's "Ultimate Concern," your overarching priority.

PUSH YOURSELF INTO THE UNKNOWN.

Take on new projects that stretch your talents. Enroll in challenging courses that add to your skillset. Volunteer for daunting projects that others might avoid. You'll earn credibility—and grit.

One of the players Q4 approached with was Langston Galloway, a sneakerhead just like Q, who'd started at the bottom and clawed his way into the NBA, playing for the New York Knicks, Detroit Pistons, and Phoenix Suns.

"**We're doing something new,**" Q said. "You tell us what you want."

"I can have my own shoe?" Q recalled Galloway saying. "I get to pick everything?"

"You got it," Q said.

Q4 sports soon gained traction with more NBA athletes, as well as those in the NFL, MLB, WNBA, and more—in 2019, a pair of customized Q4 LG9's had become so popular that they were sent to the Naismith Basketball Hall of Fame. By 2023, after six years in business, Q4 planned to expand into apparel and 3D-printed shoes.

"In the next five to ten years," Q said, "I see the footwear industry headed in a more 'bespoke' and 'niche' direction." He also believes more attention will be given to e-sports stars and gamers. Athletes on virtual courts will have their own shoes, too.

Q asserts that, "Some trends will be recycled, but the evolution of technology will bring in more innovative ways to serve new product to hungry consumers."

Last year, Q was invited to return to SCAD to help launch a new minor in sneaker design. The minor would feature courses in sketching, rendering, concept development, design, digital prototyping, and branding for luxury and high-performance sneakers: skills that shaped Q's career and turned him into a true warrior. He was also hired to teach sneaker design classes, splitting his time between SCAD Atlanta and Q4's headquarters in LA. Q joins a roster of SCAD alumni who are champions in the sneaker industry, working at Nike, Adidas, New Balance, Skechers, and more.

At Q4, his team's mantra is "Work4Yours."

BE THE WARRIOR

"What they say is impossible today, you make possible tomorrow."

— Quintin Williams

Those who tell the stories rule the world.

— Hopi proverb

5

The Storyteller

After she earned two degrees in six years, Cameron looked forward to her first professional job. She'd earned bachelor's and master's degrees in architecture and loved strategic planning and project management. Her education, she knew, had prepared her for leadership and creative roles across a variety of design disciplines. She loved making and building and she possessed a keen operational mind. But just as she was about to embark upon her design career, life intervened.

Her husband, a US Army Ranger, broke the news: they were being transferred to Camp Merrill in the mountains near Dahlonega, Georgia — a rural base, far from the design job she hoped would be hers. Given that military families move, on average, every three years, Cameron had always known this could happen, but she didn't want to let go of her design dreams so easily. Life as a military spouse had given Cameron true grit, and she was not one to give up at the first sign of hardship.

She began conspiring with Lisa, another military spouse. Both women wrestled with the paradox: how do you have a career and contribute your talents to the world, while moving around the country into new communities and new job markets? Due to being continually uprooted and the complexities of childcare (especially during deployment), military spouses have a hard time finding suitable employment — and many stop trying. And yet, military spouses "are more likely to have finished high school and have a college education than their civilian counterparts," a recent RAND study reports. "On paper, military spouses should be more employable, not less," notes the military journalist Wes O' Donnell.

Cameron and Lisa didn't want to work for someone else, only to have to pull up stakes and start all over again in a new town and a new base in a couple of years. This was a few years before COVID-19 normalized the remote office — i.e., their options were few — but limited choices do not deter entrepreneurs. Entrepreneurs love a challenge.

"And that's when R.Riveter was born," said Cameron.
The plan was to design and build not just beautiful bags but appealing and durable bags and accessories for women. So many people they knew, especially moms, would go through cheaper, less sturdy bags too quickly. They would upcycle materials — when possible they use surplus military materials, such as old tents and discarded uniforms — into sturdy handbags, crossbody bags, totes, and more. Their brand name, R.Riveter, is a direct reference to Rosie the Riveter, a World War II-era character that represented women's contributions to the war effort, such as making munitions and building aircraft. The connection to Rosie expressed their (and their products') toughness and resilience, while simultaneously communicating their personal connection to the US military. The name told a powerful story: clear, compelling, and it established an instant bond with their customers.

As demand grew, Cameron and Lisa brought on more military spouses to help with the sewing and stitching, work that these new employees, called "Remote Riveters," could complete anywhere, from any new station assignment. Cameron's and Lisa's young startup now had an even **greater purpose** than creating and selling high-quality bags: "to provide mobile, flexible income to military spouses."

Cameron said her two architecture degrees (BFA and MArch) served as excellent preparation for the launching of a new company, largely because her creative education helped her master the art of visually presenting concepts. "Right out of the gate, people thought we were bigger than we were just because of the way we were able to present the brand," she said.

In 2016, five productive years after launching, they got a huge break that would take R.Riveter to the next level: they were invited onto ABC's long-running series *Shark Tank* to pitch their ideas to angel investors and an audience of millions.

They prepared their presentation. They sought feedback from coaches. They rehearsed their story, threading their own personal journeys and professional aspirations together with the needs of so many working mothers and military spouses. In their episode, which first aired on February 5, 2016, you can sense their resolve, their passion, and their ambition to take R.Riveter national.

During the pitch, upon hearing their story — and their return on investment (almost $300,000 in sales by that point, with only an initial investment of $9,000) — billionaire Mark Cuban broke out in applause! Regarding the ingenuity of the Remote Riveters business model, Cuban said it could be "the future of manufacturing." The pandemic would happen only four years later. How prescient that statement was!

After wowing the Sharks and receiving multiple offers, Cameron and Lisa accepted Cuban's investment offer of $100,000 and 20% equity. Orders increased wildly after the episode aired. In the six years following the episode, they received continual media coverage which helped fuel the growth of their company. By 2022, they had a new flagship store in Southern Pines, North Carolina — serving as both retail outlet and design lab — and they had nearly one hundred Remote Riveters working from sea to shining sea. This success was made possible largely due to Cameron's and Lisa's intention and resolve to tell their story: in person, through highly polished pitches, as well as via superior branding and engagement across platforms.

THE WORLD'S GREATEST STORYTELLING TOOL

At some point in their careers, all creative pros must tell many stories — introverts and extroverts alike — to pitch their ideas and inventions for anyone and everyone under the sun: investors, agents, producers, podcast audiences, clients, colleagues, social media followers, and beyond. The secret art of storytelling, once the province of shamans and scribes, is now required of us all, to some degree. Each of us has a story to tell, a hero's journey describing memories, hardships, triumphs, and transformations. The story of this journey answers those all-important questions: Where did we come from? Who are we now? Our companies and brands have stories, too, about their origins and purposes. As with R.Riveter, a brand's story explains why the company exists, why it matters, what it creates, and for whom. **Why does the world need this product, this service?** Answer that question and you have your story.

Those who know how to find the story and share it with passion and poetry can open hearts and doors. It all starts with the greatest storytelling tool ever developed in the history of the world: the voice. Yet we know that the vast majority of Gen Z members often struggle with speaking anxiety, likely the result of advancements in communication technology, where text-based communication is preferred over live or in-person formats. A recent SCAD survey of the employers of our graduates — including Gensler (the world's largest architecture firm), IBM, Universal, Cartoon Network, Target, and others — found that those brands desperately need and want to hire **talent who can communicate with confidence and clarity** in a variety of contexts. Those companies voiced their desire to hire talent with "great presentation skills," "strong pitches," and "superb social interaction fluency."

 **In the knowledge economy, the power to communicate is the greatest power of all.**

Throughout their life, the aspiring entrepreneur will be called upon to speak publicly in many contexts, including: critiques in college courses (where you'll present your work and invite feedback from professors and classmates); pitch meetings (where, for example, you'll speak with investors, executives, and others about your ideas); and major keynote presentations (at conferences, festivals, and more, for audiences of hundreds or even thousands). Fret not! By the time you stand before an audience that large, you'll be a master in your discipline and highly experienced at storytelling and communication.

To begin achieving that mastery now, follow these **four pro-tips** the next time you're invited to speak before an audience:

Captivate your audience. No matter what you've been asked to say, find a way to embed your content within an engaging anecdote or series of examples. A recent study demonstrates that when speakers share only facts, audiences retain a mere 10% of the information, whereas retention jumps to 70% when facts are married with stories. Audiences tolerate (and forget) lectures. They adore (and remember) stories.

Obsess, a little. Rehearse, rehearse, rehearse! Whether you're presenting a research paper in art history class or presenting one of your filmmaking heroes with a Lifetime Achievement Award at the SCAD Savannah Film Festival (which students are selected to do!), make time to practice. If you can schedule time to rehearse in the actual space where the event will take place, all the better. Rehearsal and preparation demonstrate respect for your audience.

Abbreviate thyself. Shorter is sweeter. Try to keep most of your presentations under 10 minutes, as the experts at TED advise. Time your rehearsals the way runners track laps: beat your personal best! Curate compelling content and eliminate empty calories. Never in the history of public speaking has an audience complained about a presentation or pitch being too short.

Stand up. In a post-pandemic world, many of us find ourselves addressing audiences over Zoom as much as in person. (A recent guest of SCAD TVfest, a highly accomplished producer, explained that most of her network pitches now happen virtually.) Resist the temptation to sit during a Zoom presentation. When you stand, in rooms and Zooms, audiences feel the energy in your voice, because, as studies have found, upright speakers project authority and trustworthiness. And don't forget to smile! Remember this acronym: A.B.C. (Always Be Cheesin'). Smiles make for bright eyes!

You can bet Cameron and Lisa followed each of these pro-tips to nail their legendary Shark Tank pitch. Google "R.Riveter Shark Tank episode" and see for yourself. While they have plenty of compelling facts to share — about their sales and growth — their origin story about military spouses-turned-entrepreneurs captivates the investors (#1). Their poise and confidence attest to the diligent refinement and rehearsing of their presentation until it was sharper than an industrial sewing machine needle (#2). The entire pitch – including Q&A with the investors – lasts barely over five minutes (#3). Their physical presence radiates competence (#4).

SHOW AND TELL, TELL AND SHOW

Great writers follow a classic truism: "Show, don't tell." In other words, when narrating a story, instead of describing a moment with tiresome exposition, invite your readers into the moment with vivid scenic detail. Employ sound, smell, taste, touch, and especially powerful images to captivate your audience. For our purposes, we amend this maxim to "Show and tell." A powerfully told story will enchant your audience during a pitch or a presentation, but go further: **show striking, memorable, and highly curated images to help tell your story, and your audience won't be able to look away**.

By the time most students arrive at university, they've become quite fluent in one or more software platforms to build a beautiful "deck" (i.e., what most pros call a visual presentation), including Keynote, PowerPoint, Adobe Creative Cloud, and Google Slides. If these programs are new to you, fear not: they're intuitively designed and quick to learn for those searching out new fonts, inserting images and videos, and changing colors. At SCAD, 90% of our courses require one or more visual presentations, even for first-year students. By graduation day, SCAD students are more than fluent in building memorable decks and carry this skill directly into their new careers, ready on day one to stand up, speak up, and share beautiful images that help tell a story.

We'll add a bonus tip here, too, which bears special emphasis in a time in history when the classroom and the workplace have become more casual than ever: speakers should always look their best. The most compelling visual of all is having a professional appearance. Looking great creates confidence and conveys professionalism. Project personality and make yourself memorable through your appealing demeanor, professional appearance, and persuasive presentation. Present your best self.

6 PRO-TIPS TO SHOW YOUR STORY

1. CUT

As Coco Chanel once said, "Before you leave the house, look in the mirror and take one thing off." The same is true for your deck. Don't use three images where one will do.

2. CONNECT

Images communicate emotions that transcend the brain's language centers. Choose images that foster positive feelings. Show your audience images of what they love, and they'll love what you have to say.

3. CURATE

Refrain, when possible, from using stock images. Create your own visuals and shoot your own photographs—or find a partner who can! Show people something they've never seen before.

4. CROP

Apply the "rule of thirds" to create appealing compositions. In your mind's eye, divide an image into thirds, both horizontally and vertically. Don't remove important visual info when cropping.

5. CORRECT

Proofread once, twice, and three more times. Words are visual elements, too, and unfortunate typos (or inconsistent font styles and sizes) in a presentation distract like lint on a jacket.

6. ENHANCE

Never, ever read directly off your slides. Bold or highlight key words from the quote and paraphrase it while your audience reads. Say what you're not showing and show what you're not saying.

ON FINDING YOUR VOICE

"Humans," as writer Jonathan Gottschall says, "are storytelling animals." Novelists and scientists agree that our ability to communicate — to employ written and spoken language to describe, express, and urge others to empathy and action — is perhaps the single greatest wonder of our species, what distinguishes us from all other creatures that roam this wondrous planet. Storytelling has made civilization possible.

And yet, so many of us find our own "stories" impossible to understand, often because those narratives that have shaped us, from childhood to the present, are buried so deeply in memory and the unconscious. Your story comprises whole realms of memory and fact: who you are (personality); where you came from (home, family, place); the battles you've fought and won (conflict); why you get up in the morning (purpose). For all you aspiring entrepreneurs and inventors, the companies, brands, products, and services you long to create come from somewhere: a need in the market, yes, but also a need within you.

 **Understanding your own life — i.e., the forces and experiences that have shaped you — emboldens you to seize your calling, your purpose, your place in the world.**

By her early thirties, Mashama Bailey had mastered the art of cooking, earning her reputation in kitchens across Manhattan, from the Plaza Hotel's Oak Room to Prune on the Lower East Side. Her star was on the rise. She began to consider the possibility of running her own kitchen, and, as writer Amy Bowers noted in the *Los Angeles Review of Books*, she even opened "a supper club in Queens at her grandma's house as a way to explore and imagine the restaurant she hoped to open one day." Bailey loved to tell a story with food, exploring the past, new regions, new flavors.

"Restaurants play a big part in changing people's perspectives. Eating humanizes," Bailey writes in the book she coauthored with her business partner, John O. Morisano. "When you're sitting across the table from someone, it's easier to see your similarities than your differences." As a Black woman with roots in Savannah, Georgia, where she'd lived as a child, Bailey experienced racism both in the American South and more cosmopolitan environments in the Northeast. She felt called to tell the stories of America's past through food. "With so many restaurants in America and all the different people who have migrated here from around the world, and all of us being exposed to each other's cultures through food," Bailey asks in her book, "why is our society so divided?"

Bailey received a call one day from a fellow New Yorker, entrepreneur John O. Morisano — a call that changed her life forever. He'd just bought a dilapidated and abandoned Greyhound bus terminal in Savannah, and invited her to move back down South and join him as a partner. He wanted to call it The Grey.

The symbolism of their partnership — a white man from New York and a Black woman with Southern roots — spoke as loudly as the symbolism of the building location itself. "The terminal is located in a no-man's-land between the touristy downtown and the African American neighborhoods on the outskirts," Amy Bowers writes in her article. Morisano wanted Bailey to helm the kitchen as a co-owner and "to explore new stories in a space shaped by discrimination, with segregated waiting rooms, bathrooms, and lunch counters." Bailey jumped at the opportunity, heading south with her life and her dreams. She wanted to prove to herself, she noted in her book, "that Black American food is more than what people expect it to be. I wanted to show its value."

Within months of opening in late 2014, The Grey was named one of *Esquire*'s Best New Restaurants. "The best Southern food in the South is in Savannah, Georgia," the magazine said. Bailey had arrived, or so it seemed. As executive chef and partner, she was no longer merely running a kitchen: she was now a face — the face — of one of the hottest restaurants in the US. All eyes were on her. Every table was full, crowded with hungry pilgrims who'd made the trip just to eat Bailey's food. Critics, reviewers, writers, producers, celebrities filled the seats. "Stepping into one's power was essential as Bailey sought not to recreate recipes from the past but to 'create new dishes that are personal and invoke memory'," Bowers writes. To create these dishes, Bailey was compelled to dive deep into her own memories and stories — about family, prejudice, ambition, comfort, pain.

As she describes in *The Black, the White, and The Grey: The Story of an Unexpected Friendship and a Beloved Restaurant* (coauthored with Morisano), in those early years in Savannah, she unearthed great heaps of anger in herself — anger at America, at the South, at herself, even at her business partner. "Since returning to Savannah to open The Grey, I have stepped back and looked at how much Black people have influenced all things American, and food is no exception," Bailey noted. "Racism has been baked into the clay and cast-iron pots of the cooking across this country. It took moving back to Savannah for me to realize that I'd long suppressed those feelings of rage."

In The Grey's first few years of operation, with each new dish and each new entrepreneurial hurdle, Bailey explored old wounds and found healing. More than healing, even: **she found her voice** in all its layered, storied complexity. She discovered that she was more than a celebrated chef. She was a teller of stories, a keeper of history, a healer of division, a woman with a calling. In many ways, this discovery of her true power and purpose is what has elevated her career and her restaurant to the very zenith of the American dining scene.

A mere eight years after the restaurant's opening, The Grey has risen to iconic status, called "one of America's most important restaurants" (*Esquire*) and "one of the 100 best places in the world" (*Time*). It has been named a best restaurant by *Food & Wine*, *Eater*, and others, in addition to being featured on *Chef's Table* (Netflix) and *Top Chef*. In 2022, Bailey won the James Beard Award for Outstanding Chef, the Pulitzer Prize of cooking. Just like the founders of R.Riveter and so many others in this book — Patagonia's Yvon Chouinard, Mini City's India Jha, The Big Favorite's Eleanor Turner — Mashama Bailey found her voice and professional success by weaving her worldview and deepest concerns into her work.

You live within many narratives and journeys, past and future: of your history, your family, your education, your career, the companies and creations you hope to launch into the world. Each of these, together, comprise the Story of You. The world wants to hear your voice and to be moved by your work — whether in a book, a screenplay, a TikTok channel, a classroom presentation, a live pitch on national television, or even on a menu.

BE THE STORYTELLER

Where will you tell your story?

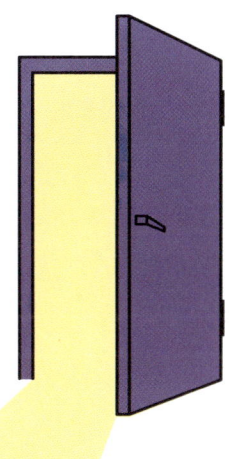

Where there is no vision, the people perish.

— The Book of Proverbs

6

The Shepherd

I n fifth grade, as his friends dreamt of becoming the next Cal Ripken or Greg Maddux, young Jett yearned to be the next Irv Kershner.

"Who's that?" his friends said.

"Director of *The Empire Strikes Back*," Jett said.

At an age when most of his friends focused on little but bikes and baseball cards, Jett imagined a future in film. "I got really into movies — I had all the Star Wars and Indiana Jones and Terminator movies on repeat — and knew I wanted to be in the industry." The eleven-year-old even begged his parents in vain to buy him a copy of *Pulp Fiction*.

In junior high, Jett made dioramas come to life through the viewfinder of his father's video camera. He and his friend Phil lensed a spoof of nature documentaries; they animated toy animals via swooping camera shots and clever editing on Apple's latest marvel, the lollipop-colored iMac. Jett's natural inclination to go beyond the assignment, to exceed the job description, was already evident.

His father ran a thriving chain of luggage stores. "With my dad owning his own company, I assumed I would someday have a business of my own," Jett said, "To me, being a boss, it's just what you do. The entrepreneurial spirit has been with me from very early on." Inspired by his father's brand-building, the young entrepreneur invented production companies for his own films. "The idea of creating a corporate identity or some kind of brand was always really interesting to me."

Because they loved James Bond movies, Jett and a friend founded Spy Club, complete with a logo and business cards. Then, in high school, Jett found his first dream job.

"I joke that Blockbuster was the best job I ever had," he said, because it allowed him to talk cinema with film buffs all day, learning his future craft. (Taking advantage of every opportunity to learn happens to be the hallmark of any effective leader.)

Jett dreamed of Oscars and Sundance screenings. When it came time for university, he had but one plan: earn a BFA in film and TV. In college, he met others who loved film just as passionately as he did, and new friends who brought complementary specialty skills to the table: sound design, set-building, screenwriting. No sooner had freshmen orientation ended than Jett was already building a new team.

Jett found many close collaborators during his undergrad years, friends who banded together to coordinate film projects on campus. They engaged in friendly competition with a rival student-run production company, the Dandy Dwarves. "Dueling producers," Jett joked, "We were like warring factions!"

Jett's group named itself Team G, after the elite military force in a screenplay written by his friend Trey Hock. Building the Team G brand, a logical extension of Spy Club and other childhood ventures, came naturally to Jett.

Jett directed his own film, *Flying Machines,* and discovered what he loved most about working with a team was the team itself: **he found satisfaction in banding together to achieve a shared outcome**. Jett found that he had a gift for encouragement and identifying his creative collaborators' secret talents. This served to further reveal his true hidden strength: he excelled at producing, even more so than directing. During his senior year, he helped nine of his classmates complete their senior thesis films. His contributions were varied and many: identifying the right cinematographer for a given project or the best sound engineer or the ideal location. Jett was beginning to discover that he was meant to be a shepherd.

GROWING THE FLOCK

In this book, we've explored the primary archetypes of the creative entrepreneur. Some are driven by ideas (The Believer), while others are driven by the grind (The Warrior) or their outsider status (The Hacker). Entrepreneurs may be naturally gifted at building networks (The Ally) or demonstrate a mastery of brand communication (The Storyteller). While you likely exemplify several of these traits in a distinct alchemy all your own, one quality demanded of all entrepreneurs is **the ability to lead**.

Every group of inventive creatives, no matter how brilliant, needs someone to guide them toward their organization's vision and outcomes, protect them from external pressures, and help them discover their own latent strengths so that everyone on the team can shine as brightly as possible. A shepherd ensures everyone understands what the team needs to accomplish and work in unity to achieve that outcome.

When you first hang your shingle, working alone, it's easy to keep the organization on one page. But say you add another employee. Now you become an educator, teaching the organization's mission, brand, and culture to your new hire. Add more. Hire a sales force, a marketing team, a few tech wizards, product managers, a creative director. Now you have a small flock. They don't all think like you — that's good: you need diversity! — and nor do they understand the company as well as you — which is the leader's task to remedy.

 **As a team grows, so does the complexity of a shepherd's work. The Boston Consulting Group's "index of complicatedness" of major companies has risen by nearly 7% per year for decades.**

As an organization grows in increasing degrees of complicated-ness, companies rely on their shepherds' leadership to clarify the brand message for their employees and consumers. As your startup grows – its structure gets more complex and processes and proce-dures multiply – you can no longer devote all of your time to dreaming up grand ideas and plans. Employees need shepherds to set expecta-tions, set the tone, and set work in motion: everything a good producer does.

 **Shepherds must unite their teams, gently guiding them toward common goals.**

At university, Jett supported classmates with their films however he could, and students clamored to join and collaborate with Team G. One student film so enthralled Jett that he stayed in town a year after grad-uation to fulfill his producer role on the project and see it to completion. *The Execution of Solomon Harris,* only eight minutes long, depicts a painful malfunction during a state-sponsored execution and wrestles with the morality of capital punishment. The short features an elaborate set built, thanks to much legwork on Jett's part, in an old prison.

The film was selected to play at the ZINEBI film festival in Spain, where Jett and his classmate-collaborators, Wyatt and Ed, saved money by staying in a hostel near the festival site. While in Spain, hang-ing out in their small room, they received the dream call: *Solomon Harris* had been selected for the Sundance Film Festival.

"We went crazy!" Jett said. "To get that call overseas...it was unbelievable."

Much of his early success – hardly a year out of college – is attribut-able to Jett's gift "for helping other people accomplish their goals, focus their vision, and get projects across the finish line." In the language of organizational management, Jett exemplifies a type of manager known as a connector. Connectors provide feedback in their area of expertise, but also understand their limitations and connect employees to others in the organization to address specific needs. Jett was a proven leader, but where could he find his next team? After a magical week at Sundance — held each year in Park City, Utah — he headed to the West Coast.

TO MOVE UP, GET LOW

In Hollywood, joined by college pals with whom he'd developed lifelong friendships, Jett and his new studio startup — called Team G, naturally! — began producing ads, shorts, and music videos for artists like Jenny Lewis and the British rock band FOALS.

However, work for Team G was sporadic. He needed to expand his network and build new alliances, and so Jett jumped at an internship offer from Roman Coppola, son of Hollywood legend Francis Ford Coppola and brother of Sophia Coppola, an accomplished director in her own right. At his production company, The Directors Bureau, Roman produced and directed music videos for The Strokes, Kylie Minogue, Beastie Boys, and others, and produced movies such as *The Darjeeling Limited* and *Fantastic Mr. Fox*. If Jett needed access to an influential network, here was his way in.

After interning for a few months, Jett soon moved up to a full-time, bottom-of-the-totem-pole gig at The Directors Bureau. He did grunt work such as ordering office supplies and answering phones. Like so many others described in this book, Jett continued to build his entrepreneurial dream by becoming an intrapreneur — **working within an established brand to learn the ropes from the inside**. Undeterred by his humble role, Jett applied himself like a boss — as if he himself were running the company. "Every project can be cool if you pour enough love into it," he said.

Jett calls this willingness to volunteer for everything the "filmmaker mentality." "It's something I look for now in my own employees," he said, "Even when I was just an intern, I was sniffing around at every project that came through the office."

Most leaders aren't hired straight into the C-suite. They start at the bottom — and make the most of the opportunity. "Grunting now will make you a better boss later. The more you know about how to do any task in your organization or line of business, the better," writes career expert Lindsey Pollak.

Mailroom-to-boardroom success stories abound. GM's chair and CEO started on the assembly line. The CEO of Walmart started out loading trucks. The CEO of Disney was a local weatherman, far from Cinderella's castle.

The best leaders understand their companies from the ground up, often because they've mastered every level of work, a journey that builds empathy. Some 84% of CEOs believe empathy drives better outcomes, and 72% of workers think empathetic leaders increase motivation. Developing empathy early pays dividends later.

Jett involved himself in all aspects of the business. "I was at the crossroads — every phone call that came in, every email went through me."

He made himself useful. "Anything they were working on that I thought was interesting — a music video, a commercial, a short film — I would offer to help, coordinate, or production manage. I would come in on weekends." Jett embraced the grind. When new projects arrived, Jett was ready to assist. He chipped in on small music videos as a production assistant, fetching coffee, finding props, copying scripts. Self-effacing, quick to deflect credit, and reluctant to rest on the laurels of past successes (Sundance, anyone?), Jett never turned down assignments or considered himself too important for any job. He exudes humility.

Deanna deBara writes that humility makes leaders approachable and "leads to **better listening, increased collaboration, and a more compassionate leadership style**. These qualities lead to better outcomes, both for the leaders and their teams." But humility doesn't mean a lack of confidence: "[Humble leaders] know their blind spots and where they may fall short — and aren't embarrassed or ashamed to admit it," deBara notes.

Not long after Jett left The Director's Bureau, he was approached by actress Lake Bell to produce a short film she had written, "Worst Enemy." When Bell had asked a Sundance organizer to recommend a producer, her contact recommended Jett. Bell's contact remembered the producer of *Solomon Harris* as a rising star. Jett and Team G would then produce In a *World...*, Bell's first full-length feature. It was widely praised as one of the funniest indie films of the 2010s. Jett had produced a feature comedy praised by A. O. Scott in the *New York Times:* another dream checked off the list.

Jett's humility and hard work earned him a reputation that impressed colleagues and would lead to further opportunities. Lana Kim, an executive producer at The Directors Bureau, enlisted Jett when she was ready to set up her own shop. She knew Jett was the kind of partner she needed: a leader with an undeniable gift for shepherding a veritable herd of talented creatives. Jett had been leading all his life! They'd run everything together. Jett didn't think twice. This is what he'd always wanted.

CHASING THE LIGHT, ONE STAR AT A TIME

Every successful creative entrepreneur knows their industry from top to bottom. The product designer must understand production, concepting, 3D modeling. The app developer must possess a mastery of coding and user experience research. The architect requires knowledge of calculus, structural engineering, and the history of the building arts, both classical and contemporary. But shepherds must go further. They must understand people. Consider entrepreneur Gary Wang. When Wang set out to create Light Chaser Animation, a new studio in Beijing based on the Pixar model, he first had difficulty finding the right people. Few large-scale animated movies were being made in Asia at the time, forcing Wang to look farther afield for talent. **To grow his flock, he would have to go hunting**. Wang traveled to the US and built a team that included a former director from Pixar and a former DreamWorks artist, both of whom helped recruit new talent from their networks.

As Wang built Light Chaser, he knew the most important thing he could do as a shepherd was to instill a common vision at the company. "It's not just my vision alone, it's all of us, so I think that's the single most important lesson I have learned," he told journalist Chris Howells.

For a leader dealing with varying personalities, writes management expert Devora Zack, flexibility is key. "Flexing your style means being versatile in how you lead, communicate, and motivate. A tough approach propels one employee; mild-mannered encouragement inspires another." (Empathy and listening skills to the rescue!) "Being flexible requires proficiency in a range of techniques, to draw upon as needed," she writes — and good leadership means building relationships with your employees. Results and relationships are intertwined, even inseparable."

Today, Light Chaser Animation is a diverse and thriving studio, with talent from many different countries and cultures. Experienced team leaders from the US, said Wang, meld well with younger animators from Beijing, many of whom studied in the States. Diversity in experience and background are fine, so long as everyone hired has the chops to produce great work.

 **"If you hire 'A' class people, they will hire 'A' class people from that point on,"** Wang said.

"If you hire 'B' class people [...] it will just go downhill from there. So we want to find our 'A' class people." Drive and desire matter. **The most important job qualification is passion**, according to Wang's executive assistant Zhongrui Yin. Speaking to *Forbes Asia*, Yin said that light chaser had "turned away talented people who see animation production more as a routine job."

THE "G" STANDS FOR GRAMMY

In 2012, six years after his graduation from SCAD, Jett and his Directors Bureau colleague Lana Kim teamed up to create their own production company, Ways & Means (W&M), whose work defied description from the first. "We started to specialize in all the stuff that was weird," Jett said. The video to promote singer-songwriter Jenny Lewis's album, *On the Line,* features a wobbly VHS recording of a psychic answering callers' questions with wacky tarot readings. *The Nowhere Inn* is a mockumentary in which musicians St. Vincent and Carrie Brownstein play versions of themselves, as St. Vincent gradually loses herself inside her own artistic persona.

When Jett paused to consider his success, he could hardly believe it: he was an executive producer at his own studio, working with some of the biggest names in the entertainment industry. He shined as a leader in W&M's first years: recruiting and hiring staff, managing the daily affairs of cast and crew, and cultivating a work environment that fosters goodwill, builds esprit de corps, and meets the needs of a complex, multifaceted collaborative film project. His team cranked out roughly seventy-five commercial projects a year, and W&M grew to a full-time staff of nine, with the addition of as many as sixty cast and crew members per project.

 How is Jett able to juggle the multitude of talent and marshal their unique competencies and technological resources to create W&M's signature content?

Because he made the classic shepherd's journey from video store clerk to phone-answerer and more, he always learned how organizations run from the inside out before taking his shot to run one of his own.

Shepherding has worked very well for Jett Steiger. His trophy case runneth over. In 2013, his work on "Up in the Air" by 30 Seconds to Mars garnered an MTV Video Music Award for Best Rock Video. In 2014, he took home a BET Award for Video of the Year for Pharrell's ubiquitous hit "Happy," which won Jett a Grammy for Best Music Video in 2015. The list goes on. **Jett attributes it all to his team**. His client roster now includes Apple, Beats by Dre, Coca-Cola, Dior, Dropbox, Facebook, Fender, GMC, Google, Jimmy Choo, Levi's, The Museum of Modern Art, Nike, Powerade, and SONOS, among others. Most recently, W&M produced a short film for Netflix celebrating the company's twenty-fifth anniversary.

"The most valuable things have been finding people that you love to work with and surrounding yourself with those people," said Jett, who collaborates with his SCAD friends to this day. "Making content is a team activity, so you need to have trust in the people you're collaborating with," he said. "Finding likeminded people is the most valuable thing you can do."

THE GOOD SHEPHERD

Successful shepherds come in all shapes and sizes. You may have some trepidation about discovering the leader within you — especially if you don't fit the stereotype of the outgoing, vociferous, larger-than-life CEO. Remember the David and Goliath story? David was a young shepherd himself, before he slew the giant.

Leading your own company can feel a bit like slaying a giant, and humility is key. Daniel Ek, founder and CEO of Spotify (another of Jett's clients!), a company worth $30 billion, describes himself as an introvert. Time and time again, studies demonstrate that **two key introvert traits — listening to others and quiet reflection — are absolutely essential to strong leadership**. Researcher Karl Moore reports that about a third of senior executives describe themselves as introverts, with the percentage among middle and first-line managers even higher. "Introverts are much more apt to listen intently and think before jumping in with their thoughts," writes Moore, and their ability to serve as sounding boards and provide thoughtful feedback adds value.

All entrepreneurs, if they find success, will become shepherds who care for others and rally growing teams toward new horizons. In the first chapter of this book, we discussed the need to develop allies, the people who root for you, look out for you, have your interests at heart. You can't get by without them. And so we end this book with the greatest ally of all: the shepherd.

Survey your growing flock, don your woolen robe, hoist your wooden hook, and assume the mantel of leader.

BE THE SHEPHERD

Learn your business from low to high, so that, someday soon, when you've ascended the hilltop and survey the brilliant droves of talent before you, you'll possess all the skills you need to slay your giants and shepherd everyone to success.

Featured SCAD alumni

Cameron Cruse (SCAD MArch, 2011; BFA, architecture, 2010) is co-founder and COO of R.Riveter, a retailer of handbags, accessories, and home goods upcycled from used and surplus textiles. The company has redefined the traditional manufacturing process into a flexible, remote network employing military spouses. Cruse and co-founder Lisa Bradley opened their first brick-and-mortar store in 2015 and were featured on *Shark Tank* in 2016, garnering interest and financial backing from businessman and co-host Mark Cuban. Cruse has also been featured on MSNBC and CBS News.

Anna Haldewang (SCAD BFA, industrial design, 2017) is founder and CEO of InsightTRAC, a robotics technology and data services company that develops agricultural solutions for almond harvesting. Haldewang launched her first company Plan Bee while a student at SCAD, reinventing the pollination industry using the latest unmanned aerial vehicle (UAV) technology. InsightTRAC has been recognized as the 2023 FIRA Ag Robot of the Year, the 2022 World Ag Expo Top-10 New Product, and the 2021 Innovate Small Business of the Year by the state of Indiana. Haldewang has been featured by *CNN Money*, Time magazine, and at the Forbes AgTech Summit.

India Jha (SCAD BFA, graphic design, 2010) is co-founder and CEO of Mini City, a social impact startup that aims to eradicate homelessness through smart tech, sustainable design, and support services. A TEDx Spotlight Speaker, Jha previously worked for organizations including CNN, the Centers for Disease Control and Prevention, and Turner Sports before joining Atlanta Tech Village as manager of the organization's It Takes a Village Pre-Accelerator program. Mini City has been honored as a Startup World Cup Atlanta Finalist, a 2019 Startup Runway Winner, and a 2018 Startup Awards Nominee for Best Social Good Startup.

Jett Steiger (SCAD BFA, film and television, 2006) is co-founder and executive producer of the award-winning creative studio Ways & Means. Steiger's work has screened at prestigious global venues including the Sundance Film Festival, Cannes Film Festival, SXSW, Tribeca Film Festival, Toronto International Film Festival, and International Film Festival Rotterdam. His feature films include *The Nowhere Inn* (2021), *Super Dark Times* (2017), and *In a World...* (2013). Steiger has also produced campaigns for global brands like Apple, Sonos, Facebook, Levi's, Nike, and Spotify, as well as music videos for artists like BROCK-HAMPTON, Grimes, Dirty Projectors, Sam Smith, and St. Vincent. In 2015, Steiger won the Grammy Award for Best Music Video for Pharrell Williams' hit song "Happy."

Eleanor Turner (SCAD BFA, fashion, 2008) is the founder and CEO of The Big Favorite, a zero-waste clothing company taking on the excesses of fast fashion. Turner previously designed for iconic American brands including J.Crew, Tommy Hilfiger, and Tory Burch. In 2015, she cofounded Argent, a women's apparel company aimed at empowering working women through stylish and functional clothing. Featured in *Vogue*, *WWD*, *Glamour*, *The New York Times*, *The Wall Street Journal*, and *Forbes*, Turner has dressed trailblazing women such as Hillary Clinton, Lilly Singh, Emily Weiss, Kamala Harris, Amy Poehler, Awkwafina, America Ferrera, Gloria Steinem, and many others.

Quintin "Q" Williams (SCAD professor of accessory design; BFA, industrial design, 2011) is co-founder and chief global designer of the innovative sneaker company Q4 SPORTS, creating distinct, highly functional products in partnership with athletes, influencers, and entertainers. Following an internship with a private label designing for a European clientele, Williams was personally selected to attend the PENSOLE Footwear Design Academy with D'Wayne Edwards, former director of the Jordan brand. Williams has designed for professional athletes in the NFL, MLB, NBA, and WNBA in addition to freelance projects for companies including Bata, Native, and Disney.

Acknowledgments

Thank you to the SCAD designers, educators, subject matter experts, writers, and others who contributed their talents to create this book:

Paula Wallace, SCAD president and founder

Glenn Wallace (BFA, interior design, 1996), chief operating officer

Divna Bileva, associate art director

Ray Crowell, director of SCADpro Fund

Jeff Catron, senior copy editor

Harrison Scott Key (MFA, writing, 2013), executive dean

Sarah Kramer, senior editor

Ken Krattenmaker, executive writer

Jennifer McCarn (MFA, graphic design, 2002), senior art director

Chris Miller, executive director

Amelia Parkes (MFA, writing, 2019), executive researcher

James Toftness, publications manager

Anna VanDer Schaaf, executive researcher

Erin Williams, senior director of production

A very special thanks to the brilliant SCAD alumni who contributed their time, talents, and stories to help create this book:

Dominica Baird (MA, luxury & fashion management, 2015; BFA, fashion, 2002), global director of trends and VTO, Maybelline; SCAD Chair of Business of Beauty and Fragrance

Angela Benton (MFA, graphic design, 2007), CEO, Streamlytics; chief creative, Angela Benton, Inc.

Vijay Chakravarthy (MA, industrial design, 2011), practice director, service design and experience design, Philips

Cameron Cruse (BFA, architecture, 2010; prof MArch, 2011), COO and co-founder, R.Riveter

Kati Curtis (BFA, interior design, 1993), principal designer, Kati Curtis Design

Margaret Daniel (BFA, interior design, 2019), founder and president of Margaret Daniel LLC

Jocelyn DeSisto (BFA, jewelry, 2017), creative director and co-founder, Lot28

Heidi Elnora (BFA, fashion, 2002), founder and CEO, Build-A-Bride Enterprises, Inc.; founder and CEO of the Heidi Elnora Atelier

Alyson Gurney (BFA, graphic design, 2018), owner, Little Felted Friends

Anna Haldewang (BFA, industrial design, 2017), founder and CEO, InsightTRAC

India Jha (BFA, graphic design, 2010), founder, Mini City

Allan Holmes (BFA, advertising, 2012), staff interaction designer, Google (since August 2022)

Mia Kernaghan (BFA, writing, 2018), global customer experience and education, senior digital education specialist, Kiehl's

Susan Laney (BFA, photography, 1996), owner, Laney Contemporary

Jacey Lucus (BFA, graphic design, 2010), president, Community Bucket

Mike Mullan (MFA, illustration, 2010), illustrator and designer, mullanillustration.com

Jeremy Nguyen (BFA, sequential art, 2011), cartoonist, illustrator, and writer, jeremywinslife.com

Zach Parrish (BFA, animation, 2007), animation director, Netflix

Cari Clark Phelps (BFA, graphic design, 1999), CEO, Clark Creative Communications

Joseph Pruitt (MA, industrial design, 2007), CEO, Spider Grills; managing partner and CEO, Align Machine Works; CEO, Atlas PMG; founder and CTO, BetaJet

José Reyes (BFA, graphic design, 1995), executive director, principal, and founder, Metaleap Creative

Robyn Richardson (MFA, design management, 2013), senior design strategist, Booz Allen Hamilton

Alex Sander (BFA, UX design, 2018), senior product designer, Curious Creators Co.

Katherine Sandoz (MFA, painting, 2005; MFA, illustration, 1998), artist and collaborator, katherinesandoz.com

Giana Shorthouse (BFA, interior design, 2012), owner, Studio Giana

Jett Steiger (BFA, film and television, 2006), executive producer and co-founder, Ways & Means

Clay Stein (BFA, service design, 2014), senior product designer, Meta

Clay Stricklin (BFA, graphic design, 1998), senior art director/creative lead, Philips Design

Colin Tunstall (BFA, graphic design, photography, 2003), creative director and owner, Saturdays NYC

Eleanor Turner (BFA, fashion, 2008), founder and CEO, The Big Favorite; co-founder, Argent

Lou Ward (BFA, motion media design, 2014), founder and creative director, Tinker Studio; senior product designer, Reddit

Quintin "Q" Williams (SCAD professor of accessory design; BFA, industrial design, 2011); Founder, Q4 Sports

A'ndrea Wilson (MFA, dramatic writing, 2017), president, Divine Garden Press/Divine Garden Entertainment; executive producer, New Kitty Media

James Zdaniewski (BFA, computer art, 2003), director of design, Rockstar Games

Bibliography

"2017 Cone Gen Z CSR Study: How to speak Z." Cone Communications, 2017. https://conecomm.com/wp-content/uploads/2022/03/2017-Cone_CSR_GenZ_PDF.pdf

"About ALDI" https://www.aldi.us/en/about-aldi/faqs/about-aldi/

Andrews, Linda Wasmer. "To Become a Better Writer, Be a Frequent Walker." Psychology Today, March 28, 2016. https://www.psychologytoday.com/us/blog/minding-the-body/201603/become-better-writer-be-frequent-walker

Bailey, Mashama, and John O. Morisano. Black, White, and The Grey (excerpt), 2021. https://www.penguinrandomhouse.com/articles/black-white-and-the-grey-excerpt/

Bapna, Sofia, and Russell Funk. "Interventions for Improving Professional Networking for Women: Experimental Evidence from the IT Sector." March 19, 2020. https://papers.ssrn.com/sol3/papers.cfm?abstract_id=3157260

Beheshti, Naz. "Improve workplace culture with a strong mentoring program." Forbes Magazine, January 23, 2019. https://www.forbes.com/sites/nazbeheshti/2019/01/23/improve-workplace-culture-with-a-strong-mentoring-program/?sh=69e9784876b5

Bonner, Mehera. "Beyonce and Jay-Z's Combined Net Worth is Bigger than my Lil Brain Can Comprehend." Cosmopolitan Magazine, September 30, 2022. https://www.cosmopolitan.com/entertainment/a22528348/beyonce-jay-z-net-worth/

Bowers, Amy. "Building Trust: On Mashama Bailey and John O. Morisano's 'Black, White, and The Grey." Los Angeles Review of Books, October 29, 2021. https://www.lareviewofbooks.org/article/building-trust-on-mashama-bailey-and-john-o-morisanos-black-white-and-the-grey/

Box Office Mojo, "Franchise: Rocky." https://www.boxofficemojo.com/franchise/fr2840039173/?ref_=bo_frs_table_38

Brantner, Eric. "Here's how much time Americans have saved by not commuting over the last year (by city)." Makealivingwriting.com. https://makealivingwriting.com/commuting-map-remote-working/

Bredbenner, Jamie. "Generation Z: A Study of Its Workplace Communication Behaviors and Future Preferences." May 2020. https://soar.wichita.edu/bitstream/handle/10057/18832/t20008_Bredbenner.pdf?sequence=1&isAllowed=y

Brzyski, Laura. "This local fashion brand wants you to 'plant' your underwear—All for Mother Nature's sake." Philadelphia Magazine, June 7, 2022. https://www.phillymag.com/be-well-philly/2022/06/07/soil-your-undies-campaign/

"The Case for Face-to-Face." Forbes Insights, Forbes Magazine, 2009. https://images.forbes.com/forbesinsights/StudyPDFs/Business_Meetings_FaceTo-Face.pdf

"The Chinese animation firm aiming to rival Hollywood." Zhuiguang.com, August 4, 2014. http://www.zhuiguang.com/?p=409&lang=en

Clair, Michael. "Who are the Savannah Bananas?" MLB.com, June 16, 2022. https://www.mlb.com/news/savannah-bananas-the-dancing-globetrotters-of-baseball-explained

Clear, James. The Science of Developing Mental Toughness in Your Health, Work, and Life." Jamesclear.com. https://jamesclear.com/mental-toughness

Cole, Jennifer. "The best new restaurant in America 2015: The Grey." Esquire Magazine, October 13, 2015. https://www.esquire.com/food-drink/restaurants/a38811/the-grey/

Davis, Michael. "Stories—not statistics—are memorable." SpeakingCPR.com, November 7, 2015. https://speakingcpr.com/the-numbers-dont-lie-stories-not-statistics-make-you-memorable/

Debara, Deanna. "Humility in leadership: The unsung skill of great leaders." Betterup.com, March 29, 2022. https://www.betterup.com/blog/humility-in-leadership

Duckworth, Angela. "FAQ." Angeladuckworth.com, 2022. https://angeladuckworth.com/qa/

Duckworth, Angela, et al. "Grit: Perseverance and Passion for Long-Term Goals." Journal of Personality and Social Psychology 92(6), July 2007, pp. 1087-1101. DOI: 10.1037/0022-3514.92.6.1087.

Duncan, Aaron M., "Reimagining the Self-Made Man: Myth, Risk, and the Pokerization of America." Western Journal of Communication 78(1), January-February 2014, pp. 39-57. DOI: 10.1080/ 10570314.2013.807435

"The Entrepreneurial Journey." Skynova.com, 2021. https://www.skynova.com/blog/the-entrepreneurial-journey

"Entrepreneurship." Thisibelieve.org. https://thisibelieve.org/essay/135885/

Fischer, Sara. "LinkedIn aims to close the 'network gap.'" Axios.com, September 26, 2019. https://www.axios.com/2019/09/26/linkedin-inequality-network-gap-job-opportunities

Fisher, Julia Freeland. "How to get a job often comes down to one elite personal asset, and many people still don't realize it." CNBC.com, December 27, 2019, updated February 14, 2020. https://www.cnbc.com/2019/12/27/how-to-get-a-job-often-comes-down-to-one-elite-personal-asset.html

Freiberg, Kevin and Jackie. "20 Reasons Why Herb Kelleher Was One of the Most Beloved Leaders of Our Time." Forbes Magazine, January 4, 2019. https://www.forbes.com/sites/kevinandjackiefreiberg/2019/01/04/20-reasons-why-herb-kelleher-was-one-of-the-most-beloved-leaders-of-our-time/?sh=26b-0918cb311

Fuhrer, Margaret. "'Baseball Players Don't Dance'? I Beg to Differ." The New York Times, May 31, 2022. https://www.nytimes.com/2022/05/31/arts/dance/savannah-bananas-tik-tok-baseball.html

Getz, Isaac, and Laurent Marbacher. "A lesson in creating successful companies that care." Strategy-business.com, June 10, 2020. https://www.strategy-business.com/article/A-lesson-in-creating-successful-companies-that-care

Giang, Vivian. "How to manage different personality types." AmericanExpress.com, May 12, 2022. https://www.americanexpress.com/en-us/business/trends-and-insights/articles/5-ways-to-manage-different-personality-types/

Giller, Megan. "21st Century Vending: How Sprinkles' Standalone Cupcake ATM Works." Spoon.tech, October 25, 2016. https://thespoon.tech/21st-century-vending-how-sprinkles-standalone-cupcake-atm-works/

Goldstein, Phil. "Social Enterprise Mini City Uses NFC Tech to Help Homeless Population in Atlanta." BizTech Magazine, October 25, 2018. https://biztechmagazine.com/article/2018/10/social-enterprise-mini-city-uses-nfc-tech-help-homeless-population-atlanta

Gonzalez, Alden. "The most fun you can have at the ballpark? What MLB could learn from the Savannah Bananas." ESPN.com, August 19, 2022. https://www.espn.com/mlb/insider/insider/story/_/id/31589713/the-most-fun-at-ball-park-mlb-learn-savannah-bananas

Hawk, Tony. "Do What You Love." NPR.org, July 24, 2006. https://www.npr.org/2006/07/24/5568583/do-what-you-love

Joni, Saj-Nicole. "Stop Relying on Experts for Innovation: A Conversation with Karim Lakhani." Forbes Magazine, October 23, 2013. https://www.forbes.com/sites/forbesleadershipforum/2013/10/23/break-out-of-relying-on-experts-for-innovation-a-conversation-with-karim-lakhani/?sh=15e65e2194b6

Kaufman, Wendy. "A successful job search: it's all about networking." NPR.org, February 3, 2011. https://www.npr.org/2011/02/08/133474431/a-successful-job-search-its-all-about-networking

Martinuzzi, Bruna. "9 Easy Ways to Remember Your Presentation Material." Americanexpress.com, April 11, 2012. https://www.americanexpress.com/en-us/business/trends-and-insights/articles/business-by-the-book-remembering-presentation-material/

McCormick, Katie. "Quantum Music." Aeon.co, May 6, 2021. https://aeon.co/essays/uniting-the-mysterious-worlds-of-quantum-physics-and-music

McElroy, Nicole Gull. "How did Carvana make it onto the Fortune 500? Unconventional values—and car vending machines." Fortune Magazine, June 2, 2021. https://fortune.com/2021/06/02/carvana-car-vending-machines-fortune-500/

McIntyre, Georgia. "What Percentage of Small Businesses Fail? (And Other Need-to-Know Stats). Fundera by Nerdwallet, November 20, 2020. https://www.fundera.com/blog/what-percentage-of-small-businesses-fail?irclick-id=1qDxbL010xyNROdwa626QSIRUkD1RZW912tszU0&utm_campaign=Skim-bit%20Ltd._10078&utm_source=Impact&utm_content=Online%20Tracking%20Link&utm_medium=affiliate&irgwc=1

Meet Quintin Williams of Q4 Sports in Inglewood." VoyageLA, May 29, 2019. http://voyagela.com/interview/meet-quintin-williams-q4-sports-inglewood/

Meisenzhal, Mary. "Subway is straying from the business model that made it the biggest fast-food chain in the world." Business Insider, July 5, 2022. https://www.businessinsider.com/subway-is-abandoning-customized-sandwiches-for-simpler-menus-2022-7

Moore, Karl. "How introverted leaders can be better managers for their extroverted employees." Forbes Magazine, May 26, 2021. https://www.forbes.com/sites/karlmoore/2021/05/26/how-introverted-leaders-can-be-better-managers-for-their-extroverted-employees/?sh=34ae726f1eb8

Morgan, Nick. "Why you shouldn't give a presentation sitting down." Forbes Magazine, April 30, 2015. https://www.forbes.com/sites/nickmorgan/2015/04/30/why-you-shouldnt-give-a-presentation-sitting-down/?sh=1f88328d2ded

Nihill, David. "How long should your talk be? Shorter than you think." Inc.com, May 5, 2015. https://www.inc.com/david-nihill/how-long-should-your-talk-be.html

O'Donnell, Wes. "Entrepreneurship Series: R.Riveter with Founders Cameron Cruse and Lisa Bradley." American Public University EDGE, June 26, 2018. https://apuedge.com/entrepreneurship-series-r-riveter-with-founders-cameron-cruse-and-lisa-bradley/

Olito, Frank. "10 CEOs that started in extry-level positions at the companies they now lead." Business Insider, August 2, 2019. https://www.businessinsider.com/ceos-started-entry-level-at-company-2019-7

"Our Story." R.Riveter.com. https://www.rriveter.com/pages/ourstory

Perna, Mark. "Gen Z Wants to Change The World—At Your Company." Forbes Magazine, December 10, 2019. https://www.forbes.com/sites/markcperna/2019/12/10/gen-z-wants-to-change-the-world-at-your-company/?sh=79266d0d3c56

Pollak, Lindsey. "Why 'grunt work' matters." Lindseypollak.com, 2011. https://lindseypollak.com/why-grunt-work-matters/

Prossack, Ashira. "5 Traits of Highly Connected People. Forbes Magazine, December 28, 2018. https://www.forbes.com/sites/ashiraprossack1/2018/12/28/highly-connected-people-traits-networking/?sh=4da86ff65e66

Rominger, Robyn. "Navel orangeworm: A costly pest in almonds." Southeast FarmPress, May 16, 2018. https://www.farmprogress.com/tree-nuts/navel-orangeworm-costly-pest-almonds

"SCAD alumni open up about their careers." SCADdistrict.com, October 29, 2014. https://scaddistrict.com/scad-alumni-open-up-about-their-careers/ Shao, Heng. "Animation start-up 'Light Chaser' scores big hit in China with first short film." Forbes Magazine, March 27, 2014. https://www.forbes.com/sites/hengshao/2014/03/27/animation-start-up-light-chaser-scores-big-hit-in-china-with-first-short-film/?sh=3ebdb46c724a

Sheehan, Jason. "There Is No Such Thing as Too Much Barbecue." NPR.org, May 29, 2006. https://thisibelieve.org/essay/5322/

Sinek, Simon. "The Golden Circle – TedTalks 2009." Youtube.com, August 14, 2012. https://www.youtube.com/watch?v=fMOlfsR7SMQ

Torres, Roselinde, et al. "The Rewards of CEO Reflection." BGC.com, June 29, 2017. https://www.bcg.com/publications/2017/leadership-talent-people-organization-rewards-ceo-reflection

"What makes a good leader? 10 essential qualities to learn." Walden University, January 28, 2021. https://www.waldenu.edu/programs/business/resource/what-makes-a-good-leader-ten-essential-qualities-to-learn

"What's Inside the Minds of Gen Z?" Girls with Impact, 2020. https://drive.google.com/file/d/1l1sA333bB406n0Grw4W7Mc6jGrErnOsm/view

Wilde, Sari. "There are 4 types of bosses. There's the one you want to work for—and why experts say they're the most successful." CNBC.com, March 9, 2022. https://www.cnbc.com/2022/03/09/the-main-types-of-bosses-and-managers-and-the-best-one-to-work-for-according-to-career-experts.html

Wolff, Hans-Georg and Klaus Moser. "Effects of Networking on Career Success: A Longitudinal Study." Journal of Applied Psychology 94(1), February 2009. DOI: 10.1037/a0013350

Wronski, Laura. "Nine in 10 workers who have a career mentor say they are happy in their jobs." CNBC.com, July 16, 2019. https://www.cnbc.com/2019/07/16/nine-in-10-workers-who-have-a-mentor-say-they-are-happy-in-their-jobs.html

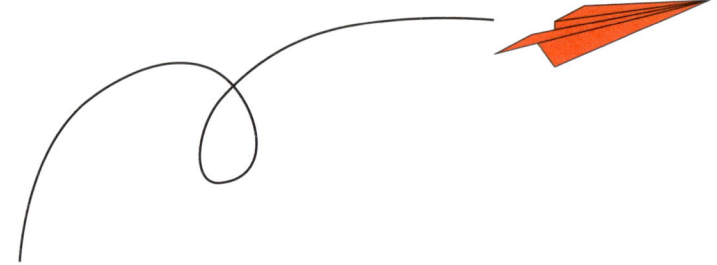

SCAD University Press
Savannah, GA 31401
scad.edu

Printed in the United States of America

Illustrations by Jeremy Nguyen

Cover design by Jeremy Nguyen

ISBN: 978-0-9601215-4-0

SCAD UNIVERSITY PRESS
Divna Bileva, associate art director
Jeff Catron, senior copy editor
Sarah Kramer, senior editor
Jennifer McCarn, senior art director
Chris Miller, executive director
James Toftness, publications manager
Erin Williams, senior director of production